THE ANGLO-SAXON CENTURY AND THE UNIFICATION OF THE ENGLISH-SPEAKING PEOPLES

LECTOR HOUSE PUBLIC DOMAIN WORKS

THE ANGLO-SAXON CENTURY AND THE UNIFICATION OF THE ENGLISH-SPEAKING PEOPLES

JOHN RANDOLPH DOS PASSOS

ISBN: 978-93-90015-24-5

Published: 1903

LECTOR HOUSE LLP
E-MAIL: lectorpublishing@gmail.com

THE ANGLO-SAXON CENTURY AND THE UNIFICATION OF THE ENG-LISH-SPEAKING PEOPLES

BY

JOHN R. DOS PASSOS

OF THE NEW YORK BAR

AUTHOR OF "STOCK BROKERS AND STOCK EXCHANGES," "THE INTERSTATE COMMERCE ACT," "COMMERCIAL TRUSTS," ETC.

SECOND EDITION

1903

CONTENTS

CHAPTER IV

CHAPTER V

CHAPTER VI

CHAPTER VII

CONCLUSION

INTRODUCTION

TO THE SECOND EDITION

I CANNOT but feel that the exhaustion of the first edition of this book so quickly, indicates that the public is, at least, interested in the questions it discusses.

. I believe that the twentieth century is *par excellence* "The Anglo-Saxon Century," in which the English-speaking peoples may lead and predominate the world. My mind recoils from any other picture, because the failure of our people to assume the power committed to their hands means the segregation of nations and states, and the general disorganisation of society through cruel, bloody, and fratricidal wars. The elimination of war and the advancement of civilisation have been the motive of my book. To effect this object I have seen no other way than to concentrate power in the hands of the most worthy. If the Anglo-Saxon peoples do not come within that denomination, what other will?

The struggle for predominance, tacit or avowed, still goes on. No one important nation, in our times, is more content to remain in a second, or even an equal place, than at any former period of history. Choice then, being necessary, what choice shall be made? The an```swer of everyone who is likely to be within the circle of my readers, and whose mind is not prepossessed by some special and, as I must think, perverse influence, may be confidently anticipated. It will be that which I have given.

I have opened up a plan which I consider feasible. I have set no time for its adoption either in whole or in part. On the contrary, I asserted (pp. 2 and 3) that "the question [of unification], in the ordinary course of events, must pass through the crucible of debate, tinctured and embittered by prejudice, ignorance, and jealousy … it may drag along through years, the sport of every whirlwind of domestic and foreign politics."

To compare small things with great, I recall that Lord Bacon advocated, in his own powerful and masterly way, the union of Scotland and England more than one hundred years before it was actually accomplished.

In launching another edition of the book upon the great sea of modern literature, I feel renewed confidence that it will eventually attract a nucleus of readers sufficient in number and influence to mould its suggestions into public issues, to be argued and disposed of, in a manner commensurate with their importance.

J. R. D. P.

August, 1903.

INTRODUCTION

IN this book I advocate the union of all the English-speaking peoples by steps natural and effective. Believing that the only real obstacle to a complete and sympathetic *entente* between the Anglo-Saxon peoples may arise from the situation of Canada, I urge her voluntary incorporation with the American Republic. Upon broad principles, this incorporation ought not to be difficult, seeing that the Federal idea, which has been so happily developed in the existing Canadian institutions, corresponds, in a large degree, with our own. As an offset, as well as to soften, if not wholly eradicate, any sentiment adverse to the surrender of a separate national existence, I propose the establishment of a common, interchangeable, citizenship between all English-speaking Nations and Colonies by the abrogation of the naturalisation laws of the United States and the British Empire, so that the citizens of each can, at will, upon landing in the other's territory, become citizens of any of the countries dominated by these Governments.

The proposition of the free admission of English and Americans to citizenship in the respective Governments of the United States and the British Empire, without a previous quarantine, is neither visionary nor impracticable; on the contrary, as I show in Chapter VII, it is in entire harmony with the spirit and purpose of the naturalisation laws, and it is, moreover, sanctioned by the authority of history and of several distinguished modern names.

To make the union permanent and indissoluble, I would introduce free trade between the United States and the British Empire, the same as exists between the several States of our Republic; and to this I would add the adoption of the same standard of money and of weights and measures. To render armed conflict impossible in the event of any differences arising between us, I would establish an Arbitration Court, with full jurisdiction to determine finally all disputes which may hereafter arise.

By these means a real and permanent consolidation of the Anglo-Saxon peoples will be accomplished, without the destruction or impairment in the least degree of the political autonomy of the individual governments of the United States or of the British Empire, and without departing from any maxims of the international policy of either.

I do not advocate, but deprecate, in common with those who have given the subject serious study, a defensive and offensive alliance, as this term is now used.

The events revealed in the history of the Anglo-Saxon peoples, and the conclusions logically deducible therefrom, amply justify the unification of the whole English-speaking family as a wise and necessary step in their destiny and progress.

I hereafter endeavour to show that such an alliance is natural; that, growing out of our mutual interests, it is necessary; and that a true analysis of our duty to ourselves and our relations to the outside world impresses it upon us as a sacred mission.

Upon these foundations I have built the structure of an enduring Anglo-Saxon league. If I am wrong in the premises, the international mansion which I have endeavoured to construct must fall to the ground. If, on the other hand, I am correct, then the two powerful motives which underlie all individual and national action are present, for *sentiment* and *selfishness* alike demand its consummation.

The general subject of an alliance of some kind has already been largely discussed in both countries, but it has taken no tangible shape beyond the formation of a few societies whose end has been to develop closer relations between the two peoples, and whose success has been, alas! most indifferent.

The opening of the twentieth century reveals two great conditions which must deeply and powerfully affect the acts of individuals and nations, and compress events, which ordinarily would take ages to mature, into a few years. First, there are no more worlds to discover, and territorial absorption by purchase or force of arms is the sole means by which the most powerful nations can add to their possessions. Diplomatic eyes now look inward and not outward. Second, all nations have become near neighbours to each other; and the achievements of science, conquering space and time, enable the newspapers, among other things, to present each morning a full picture of the doings of the whole world on the preceding day. The important acts of a nation's life are laid bare daily, and the profoundest secret of state can no longer be withheld from the lynx-eyed newsgatherer. The motives, ambitions, and actions, of the nations are thus constantly revealed to all who wish to read them in the journals, for the price of a few pennies. Marvellous! Most marvellous!

> "High placed are we, the times are dangerous,
> Grave things and fateful hang upon the least
> In nice conjunctures."[1]

Obeying the course of general progress, political and diplomatic events in this age must "therefore, take root and ripen quickly. Each nation is armed to the teeth, or is ready so to arm, and the expenditure of money for soldiers and sailors and the equipment for war will not stop on this side of national solvency and extermination. A complete justification of Anglo-Saxon aggregation grows out of the fact that it can arrest and destroy this dreadful modern tendency. But even if angels advocated it, a step of such profound importance would necessarily be preceded by much private and public argument, in which the outside world would largely participate, and from whom, perhaps, much opposition might arise; yet it may mature, forsooth, over night.

The suggestion of an Anglo-Saxon union will be looked upon with disfavour by foreign nations, and the narrow view will be urged, that by means of it, disproportioned power will be lodged in our hands to their detriment. There is no

[1] *Madalena; or The Maids' Mischief*, by Theodore McFadden.

weight, however, in the objection: power lodged in the proper hands hurts no one. Mistakes there may be here and there, but the course of this great race cannot be retarded. It must go on. It must move forward in the mission to spread Christianity and civilisation everywhere, and to open up the undeveloped part of the world to the expanding demands of commerce, and of all that commerce, liberally conducted, implies.

Let us take up together the work so magnificently performed by the United States and by England down to the commencement of this century. Once for all let prejudices be cast aside. Let us unite in a great English-speaking family. Let us be content to learn from each other. And when the curtain of the twenty-first century is raised, may the successful anglicisation of the world be revealed; may the real spirit of our institutions and laws prevail everywhere, and the English language have become the universal dialect of mankind.

In the view I have given of English history, manners, and institutions, and their relation to our own, I am aware that I do not go beyond the merest sketch. I should, perhaps, have paused longer on that part of the subject,—it would have been pleasant to do so,—but as it is practically inexhaustible, it would have changed the character of the work and have swelled it to undue proportions. I have said enough, I think, to point out the path to every intelligent reader likely to be interested in this question, and who has not heretofore made it a study. Once accepted as a subject of interest, every kind of reading, even to the most light and desultory which our copious literature affords, may be made to cast an illumination upon it. Thus, while mentioning the great leading facts of English Constitutional development—those more obvious stepping-stones upon which the race ascended in that difficult path—I have found it impossible to detail all the influences, whether of ancient or recent growth, which accompanied or produced the respective movements. The least obtrusive causes are not infrequently the most potent as well as the most interesting. I firmly believe that the ultimate ascertainable causes in all such cases will be found in the character of the people, however that character may have been generated.

I wish to acknowledge publicly, and return my thanks for, the substantial aid which I have received in the preparation of this book from my dear and life-long friend, Theodore McFadden, Esq., of the Philadelphia Bar, the author of a most exquisite and classic drama, *Madalena; or The Maids' Mischief*, and many effective essays and articles. I have discussed every part of this work with him, and in the course of its preparation, he has made many valuable suggestions, some of which I have incorporated herein in his exact language. While we are in earnest agreement as to the main purpose of the book, namely, the removal of prejudices and the approximation of the two peoples for all great and beneficial objects, including their mutual defence, our views are not always in accord as to the methods of giving effect to that purpose. To differ with one of the ripest scholars, one of the most profound and liberal thinkers and eloquent writers of the day, even upon a trivial point, is a matter of sincere regret, but convictions upon the subjects discussed herein, at first light and eradicable, have, by reflection and study, become strengthened and deepened, and I shrink not from the responsibility and duty of giving them full light.

May they bear ripe and wholesome fruit!

J. R. D. P.

NEW YORK, April, 1903.

THE ANGLO-SAXON CENTURY

CHAPTER I

TWO EVENTS WHICH MARK THE CLOSE OF THE NINETEENTH CENTURY

WHEN the sun disappeared on the last day of the Nineteenth Century, it left in the horizon vivid pictures of two unexpected and incomplete events, whose influences will penetrate far into the realm of future history and throw light upon the great records which will be made in this new century. In one picture, the United States of America was seen fighting in the Philippines for the possession of a land which she claimed by the double title of conquest and purchase. In the other, the British Empire was battling with the Boers; sending her armies over the seas into Africa, to answer the defiant and goading challenge of that people.

Strange and unexpected history! The two powers the least prepared for or anticipating war were forced into battle; while Germany, France, Austria, and Italy, armed to the teeth, momentarily expecting strife, became spectators instead of actors. We must prepare always for the unexpected.

Neither the acquisition by the United States of new territories, conquered or purchased, from a weaker power, nor the subjugation of the Boers by England and the enforcement of absolute sovereignty upon their republics, are, *per se*, events of supreme importance to the outside world.

The continental powers view with comparative complacency the relinquishment of the sovereignty of Spain over the Philippines, Cuba, and Puerto Rico; and while the subjugation of the Boers, and the metamorphosis of their republics into colonies of the British Empire, awakens keener interest and criticism, these acts will, nevertheless, pass unchallenged, and eventually be acquiesced in.

But the deep significance of these two historical incidents is, that they have brought the English-American peoples into such striking prominence that their present and future relations to each other, and the aim and scope of their ambition, separately or combined, must become an absorbing topic of international thought and discussion.

A union of all the English-speaking peoples has become a probability; and while the question, in the ordinary course of events, must pass through the crucible of debate, tinctured and embittered by prejudice, ignorance, and jealousy, a sudden upheaval or unexpected revolution in international affairs might cause its solution in a day. On the other hand, it may drag along through years, the sport of every whirlwind of domestic and foreign politics.

The Anglo-Saxon people should only be concerned with the right and wrong of the subject—absolutely fearless of the results to which an inquiry based upon sound premises may lead. It is now manifest that to this great race is entrusted the civilisation and christianisation of the world.

Whether they will perform the duties of this sacred trust is the problem of the Twentieth Century.

I shall proceed to state the grounds for this opinion, and to unfold the reasons which should influence this great people to act as one.

I.—BY THE SPANISH WAR, THE RELATIONS OF THE UNITED STATES TO EUROPE AND THE EAST WERE SUDDENLY TRANSFORMED

This war reveals the United States in many aspects as *the* leading power of the world. While her wonderful development, progress, and marvellous wealth were freely talked about and ungrudgingly acknowledged, she has, by this last war, leaped, *per saltum*, into a position among nations which will force her, *nolens volens*, to assume all the burdens and responsibilities which her new rank demands. If we look the actual situation in the face, it is impossible to escape the consequences of this dénouement. The United States has suddenly become a natural and necessary party to all great international questions; and this fact, with her increasing commercial and financial power, demands that she should be ready to second the interests of her people, who are now spreading out in all directions in search of greater wealth and wider business relations. The oceans which separate the United States from Europe and the East were once supposed to be perpetual barriers to her active participation in international questions. It was assumed that she had quite enough to do, then and for all time to come, to attend to the development of her own vast and continuous country.

The victory of Dewey at Manila, however, combined with the mighty change which has been wrought in human affairs by science, electricity, and steam, struck the scales from the eyes of the world, and, presto! she has leaped into the arena of history as the most important factor of the new century. Can this situation be made other than it is by the shibboleth of party platforms, or individual opinion? Can her progress be stayed? With as much reason we may command the flowers and the trees not to grow—bid nature stand still, and her laws not operate!

She did not seek the rank of an international power; it was evolved out of a confluence of natural conditions. She can no more cast it off than can our bodies the food of which we have partaken after it has entered into our organisms. If history teaches any lesson, it is that nations, like individuals, follow the law of their being; that in their growth and in their decline they are creatures of conditions, in which even their own volition plays but a part, and that often the smallest part.

II.—THE EFFECT OF THE WAR IN AFRICA UPON THE RELATIONS AND POWER OF ENGLAND

It has been boastingly said by her enemies, and reluctantly acknowledged by some of her friends, that England has entered upon her decline, and that a decay has set in which will destroy her power and prestige. There is nothing more absurd than this assertion. The same statements were circulated in reference to her at various periods of her past history—notably at the close of the Revolutionary War. Look into her history at that time; consult the contemporaneous writers, and we shall find them replete with gloomy and direful predictions. And yet how she gathered herself together; and in a few years how resplendent she was in military and civic glory! Her political edifice cannot be destroyed so long as reason holds its sway, because it is built upon the solid foundations of true civil liberty, which it is the aim of all people to establish and conserve. Show me anyone, not actuated by pure bigotry, who would deliberately and maliciously wish to demolish such a government!

When men band themselves together in a revolutionary purpose, it is to destroy tyranny and oppression. They do not begin revolutions with edicts against liberty and free government.

England will decline, if ever she declines, when men assail order and law, and seek to erect in their stead, as a basis of government, chaos and confusion. Her literature can never be destroyed; it will enlighten the world long after her government ceases to be. It will be the basis of a new civilisation long, long after her people cease to act together. I will not weary the reader with statistics of her material growth. They show no real, permanent decline; but they do reveal that she has fierce commercial competitors in the United States and Germany. They show that she must arouse herself to a real struggle to support her people. But no matter how this war for commercial supremacy may end, we must remember that the real greatness of a nation, or people, does not wholly consist in mere material wealth. We of North America are overlooking this important fact in our sudden and marvellous development. We are to-day, and not without some truth, called a purely "dollar nation." Our people are struggling for money, as if that were the only desideratum of life. We forget that religion, in its broad sense, liberty, justice, equality, and virtue are more important than money; they are the chains of steel which bind a free people together; mere wealth without these qualities has no preserving power: and if we lose our institutions, in their form or in their spirit, of what use will money be to us, or how will it be protected? The acquisition of wealth is legitimate, but it must not be the sole aim of the people, else they will forget their duties as citizens; and should that time come, and chaos and revolution ensue, of what use will material advantages be, even if they should survive the loss of freedom?

Remember that a government based upon gold, wealth, sordidness, must end unhappily. We must have other and higher ideals for our people.

Do not misunderstand me; I do not decry individual, and, in certain degrees, aggregate wealth. Let our citizens accumulate money "beyond the dreams of avarice." Through the natural channels open for its circulation, it will gradually flow back to the community. And overlook not the difference between real and fictitious values. Men often create paper values, which disappear like snow before the summer sun when the operations of true economic principles attack them. So long as individual or combined wealth adheres to its legitimate functions, a State is safe. When, however, it is used to corrupt or influence the judiciary; when it seeks to interfere with, or affect legislation; when it subsidises or controls the press; when it severs instead of combines society; in fine, when it is used as a *substitute for character*, the people must beware; they must quickly intervene and crush it; for the pillars of all free government will then be attacked, and they will experience an oligarchy of wealth—the worst of all oligarchies and the most destructive of individual liberty.

One word more on the subject of England's alleged material decline. In less than one year she transported in her own ships two hundred and fifty thousand soldiers to South Africa, without the loss of a single life.

No other two existing nations could have accomplished the same task; and, allowing for all drawbacks and mishaps, when the history of that war comes to be written, it will be found that, under all the circumstances, it will not be the least of ancient or modern achievements. And yet with what characteristic absence of self-glorification it has been done!

In the last century, and under the glorious reign just closed, she has been perfecting more and more her constitutional system; the various classes composing her society have been thoroughly interfused; political power has been extended to the masses, education has been disseminated, benevolent enterprise has gone hand in hand with the acquisition of wealth to an unparalleled degree. These are to be set off against any possible decline in her trade. It is hard to see how even that decline can be permanent or anything more than accidental while she retains her other possessions, and along with them the virile qualities which called them into existence.

She commences the twentieth century with undiminished glory and the prospect of increasing influence.

III.-THE PRESENT DIPLOMATIC AND POLITICAL MAP OF THE WORLD

In a little less than four years, the entire relations of the nations of the world to each other have changed. Old maps have become obsolete and valueless. The plans of diplomacy have been upset. All international combinations have been frustrated, and the nice calculations and adjustments of European statesmen are, by the unexpected results of the two, in some of their aspects, insignificant wars, thrown into confusion and perplexity, if not for ever destroyed. The diplomatic slate has been sponged clean, and new alliances and international copartnerships must be written on it.

Does it not seem plain, therefore, in the shifting of places and combinations, that the British Empire and the United States are to be the chief factors in the new historical scenes of the twentieth century?

The world is now, in a practical sense, owned or controlled by five nations: the British Empire, the United States of America, Russia, Germany, and France. China, preliminary to an eventual division of her territories, has become a ward of the preceding powers, and unless, perchance by some miracle, she steals the thunder of modern Jove, and arms her hordes with fashionable artillery and ammunition, — a most unlikely prospect, except in accord with and under the tutelage of Russia, — she can no longer be numbered as a factor in international affairs. Japan, Austria, Hungary, Turkey, Italy, Spain, Portugal, Switzerland, Belgium, Holland, Norway and Sweden, and the other small sovereignties of the world are mere satellites, revolving around these great political planets, and in due course of time destined to be attached to one or the other of them, or at least so close in sympathy with their principles as to render concert of action between them inevitable.

IV.—RUSSIA, CHINA, FRANCE—THEIR RELATIONS TO EACH OTHER AND TO THE WORLD

The Russian and Spanish races will furnish two absorbing problems of this century to Europe and the United States.

Let us take up the Russian question first.

There are to-day three great rivals in the commercial world, — the United States, England and Germany. We might add France in some branches of trade, and Japan in others. The commercial ambition of the United States will be, and that of England and Germany is, world-wide. What the natural rivalry between these powers will result in I need not undertake to predict. The laws of trade, however, are unerring, and the cheapest and best seller will eventually secure the customer. As the manufactories of England, Germany, and France close their doors before the keen business genius and competition of the Yankees, immigration to the United States will increase: a hegira of foreign labourers and mechanics will set in, which will greatly thin out, if not depopulate, the old countries of Europe of their best manufacturing ability. This result is inevitable under any conditions; but it must be regarded as separate and apart from the considerations to which allusion is hereafter made. The relations of Russia to this commercial question and to the general status of European affairs, are unique and of the deepest importance. Russia to-day is in the process of governmental and national development. She is not yet, in any complete sense, an integral, sympathetic, national whole, as are the United States, England, and Germany. Her government is still experimental. She is not yet a firm, stable, political unity, but is working with tremendous activity to build up and operate a plan of internal policy. At the same time she is developing a broad, well defined, ambitious, but not unnatural external career. She is now, as ever, grasping for contiguous territories. The *one* policy is largely dependent for success upon the *other*. If she overcomes the fires of revolution that burn within her people; if she can, in spite of the diffusion of education and the principles of liberty, maintain the particular species of arbitrary government which now exists; if she succeeds in continuing a despotism, and can present an unbroken front to the civilised powers of the world, maintaining peace and order *within*, while she asserts and sustains her policy without,—in that event the external policy of Russia may become the second, if not the first, great and absorbing question of the century. If Russia does not succeed with her people; if discontent and revolution ensue; if the present dynasty is overthrown; if a new and different, government is installed in that country, or it is split up into different governments, her power as an international factor will naturally be so weakened and reduced that she may be compelled to agree to any territorial partition or adjustment which may be eventually fixed upon by the other powers, if they act together. In shaping their commercial policies, however, it will not be prudent for the United States, England, Germany, and France to rely upon the weakness of Russia's internal government, although its overthrow is an event by no means unlikely, engaged as she is in building and sustaining a political fabric contrary to modern tendencies and modern thought, and inimical to those nations which possess them. But the powers mentioned above must assume that her internal policy will succeed, and the probabilities of such success, at least for some years to come, make it important for them to act conjointly and promptly in matters pertaining to China, South-eastern Europe and Asia. No matter how they may diverge in other questions, upon the subject of China their true interests demand joint action. Under no circumstances, at least for many years, will Russia be a general commercial rival to these four powers. She has no ambition, for instance, in the direction of Africa, now covered by England, Germany, and France; nor has she any present intention of exploiting the fields of South America or Mexico. The sphere of her external policy embraces South-eastern Europe, Asia, and China, and in these fields she has always met and been checked by Great Britain. It is an absolute, indisputable fact of history, that but for the predominating influence and power of England, Russia would to-day be the complete master of China, Turkey, Persia, and other parts of Asia—in fact, of all Asia. England, alone, might still continue to check Russia's designs on these countries, but in so doing she would be acting not only for Germany, but for the United States, hence the Eastern policy of England must be radically changed, or she must act co-operatively with the United States, France, and Germany, or with one or two of these powers. She cannot for ever continue in the unavowed invidious role of defender of Europe against this gigantic, ever-advancing, all-absorbing antagonist. But eternal gratitude is due to her from the United States and the other powers of Europe for what she has already done in this direction.

Unless some general check, such as is suggested in these pages, be applied, the dream of Peter the Great would seem to be in a fair way of fulfilment. That dream was, first, the acquisition of all Asia; second, the conquest of all Europe—the latter by the instrumentality of its own dissensions, and the playing off of the rival interests, as Austria against France, afterwards France against Germany—a state of things which has an approach to realisation at the present moment. The royal dreamer did not embrace America within the scope of his vision,—a very important and ever-growing factor in the general problem, whether for good or evil.[2]

[2] I select in this connection an extract from an article in the *North American Review*, June, 1898, by Hon. David Mills, Canadian Minister of Justice, entitled "Which shall dominate, Saxon or Slav?"

"Let us consider the aims of Russia, as shown by what she has attempted and accomplished in modern times. The Russian statesman loves conquest. With him it is a habit of mind. Russia is a great Asiatic power, employing the resources of western civilisation to further her ambitious designs. Her conquests are not the outcome of industrial enterprise. They have not sprung from the necessities of commerce. Her acquisitions have not arisen from a desire to find a profitable investment for her capital. They are due entirely to a love of dominion. In the last century, she acquired all the territory lying between her western border, and the Gulf of Bothnia, and the Baltic Sea. She acquired the greater part of Poland and the whole of Crim-Tartary. In this century she has obtained Finland from Sweden, Bessarabia and a part of Armenia from Turkey. She has acquired the Caucasus, Georgia, several provinces of Persia, and the whole country from the Caspian Sea, on the west, to the borders of China, on the east, including Samarcand, Bakhara, Khiva, and Merv, besides a large section of North-eastern China. Russia is the one great state of the world that pays no regard to her treaty obligations longer than it is convenient for her to do so. Her territories cover an area nearly three times as large as the United States, and are being constantly extended. If she finds resistance at any point upon her borders, she rests there, and pushes forward her boundaries where those upon whom she encroaches are not prepared to stay her march. What she acquires is hers absolutely, the trade of the people no less than her dominion over them. Not the slightest reliance can be put upon her promises. She regards falsehood as a legitimate weapon in diplomacy, as deceit is in war. In Afghanistan, which she declared to be outside of the sphere of Russian diplomacy, and within the sphere of diplomacy of England, she carried on constant intrigues against English authority. Her representatives sought to stir up rebellion. She endeavoured to obtain the consent of its rulers for the construction of a road that would lead to India, and for the purchase of supplies that would support an army of invasion on their march. She never gives up any purpose which she has once formed. More than eight centuries ago she marched an army of 80,000 men to conquer the Byzantine Empire, and to seize Constantinople. What she then undertook, and failed to accomplish, she has never abandoned. It has been from time to time postponed for a more fitting opportunity. She lost six great armies in the march from the Caspian to Samarcand, and two centuries elapsed from the time when she contemplated this conquest before it was consummated. If the Russian Empire holds together, she counts on the conquest of Turkey, of Persia, of India, and of China.

"If Russia succeeds in the task to which she has set herself she will hold seventeen millions of square miles of territory, and she will have under her dominion nine hundred millions of people. The fall of the British Empire is regarded by Russian statesmen as essential to the realisation of her hopes. Let me ask: What would be the position of the world, with so much territory and so many people under one ruler, wielding the power necessary to the realisation of his wishes? It is only necessary to study the commercial and industrial policy of Russia to discover that she would trample into the earth every people that might aspire to better their position or to become in any way her rivals. In every department of commerce, and in every field in which greatness might be achieved, her rulers would regard any attempt at success as an attack upon her supremacy.

"In the discussion of this question I embrace the United States as a part of the Anglo-Saxon community. I do so because, in the present position of the race, and of the work which obviously lies before it, the loss of British supremacy in the world would be scarcely less disastrous to the United States than it would be to the British Empire. It is true that the United States, under the present order of things, has room for further expansion. But the present order of things rests upon Anglo-Saxon supremacy. Even within her existing limits, she may grow for many years to come; and if Turkey, Persia, India, and China were added to the empire of Russia, the whole position of the world would be completely changed; the

In the new diplomatic advent, the United States, Germany, England, and Russia, and, perhaps, France, must be the principal factors. What shall their policy be? Undoubtedly England, the United States, and Germany would never consent to allow Russia to carry out her present ambition to become the owner of China and the other Eastern possessions, which every one knows she covets, and covets quite naturally, because her contiguity to these territories makes it of vital importance for her to obtain a predominating control there, when they pass from the weak hands in which they now rest. Moreover, the strong, despotic government of Russia is suited to Chinese education and intelligence, perhaps much more so than that which any European power could establish there. But behold the proportions and strength of the Russian Empire with China and the Chinese under her control! Does any European power look with equanimity upon such a picture? Naturally, Russia will hesitate long before she will consent to relinquish her cherished dream of eventually controlling these possessions.

It has been manifest for years that China could not take care of herself, and what little diplomacy exists in modern times has been exercised in guarding the present and future integrity of that country from the grasp of rival foreign powers. Until the late war (if the anomalous events which recently transpired in China can be correctly called a war) these diplomatic questions had really involved only England and Russia. At present, the situation is as follows: China and the East must be opened to meet the increasing commercial growth of the United States, England, Germany, and France. There are not enough customers to go round; the domain of commercial activity is too narrow; competition is becoming so close and hot, especially when the United States invades those grounds heretofore exclusively occupied by England, Germany, and France, that new territories must be found, and fresh fields of trade exposed. The doors of China must be thrown wide open to the manufacturers of all these countries, on terms of equality. The policy

---

condition of things on this continent would be revolutionised. With the power thus centred under Russian control and directed from St. Petersburg, with the valley of the Euphrates occupied by Russians devoted to agriculture, with the frontiers of that mighty Empire resting upon the Indian Ocean; and with the whole commerce of Asia in her possession, Russia would, as a natural consequence of these tremendous additions, become the dominant sea power. The Pacific Ocean would be a Russian lake, and her eastern frontiers would rest upon the western shore of North America. The British Islands would rapidly diminish in population, until the number of inhabitants would be such as the product of the soil would naturally support. The United Kingdom could no longer be a market for the breadstuffs of this continent, and European immigration to America would cease. Russia would rapidly grow in wealth and in population, but no country in the Western Hemisphere would do either; for the great markets of the world would be in the possession of a power that would use them to cripple the commerce of any state which would, in any degree, aspire to become her rival.

"In the highest sense the United States has not, and cannot have, an independent existence. Her fortune is inseparably associated with the race to which she belongs, in which her future is wrapt up, and in which she lives and moves and has her being. The unity between the United States and the British Empire is a matter both of race and growth. They touch each other, and as peoples unite and great states arise, they must be, for all great international purposes, one people."

of Russia is to delay the consummation of this event. She may at some future time be in a situation where she can occupy the disputed field against all comers. She is near the ground, and is becoming more powerful every day, in proportion as her internal policy is fixed, and her laws, religion, and government are made satisfactory to her subjects.

If all these things turn out favourably for Russia, and she can secure the co-operation of China, it is not unlikely or improbable that she will one day say to the other powers, "Hands off!" and be prepared to enforce her words.

Under these circumstances, it is the unquestionable policy of England, the United States, Germany, and France, at least so far as China is concerned, to have their relations with Russia settled at once. If Russia can maintain the *status quo* until events are ripe for her to act aggressively, it is her plain policy to do so. On the other hand, England, the United States, France, and Germany can gain nothing by the delay, but everything by quick, present, concerted action. The division of China once made, Russian ambition and diplomacy are for ever checked. Of course there is the Franco-Russian alliance. I pay no attention to it. It is a farce—a diplomatic paradox; so suicidal to France's real interest that it is liable to drop to pieces at any change in the French Ministry.

Another phase of the subject, *i.e.*, the internal condition of China.

In the aspect in which I am considering the subject, I do not think I am wrong in saying that China bears the same relation to the civilised world as the continent of America did to Europe in the fifteenth and sixteenth centuries. There are, of course, great differences—China has more people—she has a more developed internal trade, her citizens have more intelligence and certain inventive and business qualities, and there are other very material features too obvious to mention, which distinguish the Chinese from the American aborigines, but in the sense in which I am speaking, the comparison is correct. China has made no distinct advance for centuries, in a civilising direction, in the sciences and arts, in commercial and manufacturing pursuits, to say nothing of political, religious, and moral improvements, schools and eleemosynary establishments. She has stood dead-still, if she has not actually taken a step backward. As a nation, China is oblivious to anything progressive. In fact, so low is she in the scale of modern civilisation, that the United States, whose commendable policy has been to invite immigrants to her shores, has deliberately shut her doors to China, and has unceremoniously refused to receive the latter's subjects either as citizens or as travellers. In ordinary circumstances, the estimation of independent thinkers, this policy of exclusion would be intolerable, but its justification has been sustained upon the ground that the Chinese are not regarded as fit associates for American citizens, and no persons are wanted in this country who do not meet this requirement. In a word, China is out of harmony in her relations to the civilised powers. With but few exceptions her policy has been to close her doors to the outside world, to shut herself up in a shell upon the approach of strangers. China, in respect to modern development, must be opened by the corkscrew of progress. She does not respond with effervescence to the approaches of civilisation. The massacre of an ambassador of a great power, the altogether unjustifiable slaughter of helpless missionaries, invited and induced to reside there by treaty, and the turbulent confusion which reigns inside of her borders, form complete evidence of the utter incapacity of the nation for respectable, stable government. She is old, childish, helpless, and if her territories are to be opened and developed, if her people are to be educated, enlightened and made prosperous, it must be by the strong hands of the civilised powers. Of course, touching and effective arguments may be made against the right of nations forcibly and bodily to take possession of Chinese soil, and intelligent and cultivated Chinese statesmen and gifted scholars like Wu Ting-Fang, the late Chinese Ambassador to the United States, may make pathetic appeals against such a movement, based upon the superior moral and legal right of the Chinese to their own soil and government. But we must look the question fairly in the face, undisturbed and unaffected by arguments which, ordinarily, would have preponderating weight. The Indians who occupied the soil of North America, the Britons who occupied the soil of England, had the same arguments. Nothing is finer than the pictured eloquence of the Indian chiefs as they spiritedly protested against the invasion of their soil and the dispersion and extinguishment of their tribal governments. But before the march of progress and the underlying necessities of civilisation, these cries of sentiment and sympathy will not long be heard. The invincible spirit of progress must go on. Like quicksilver, it will noiselessly run into every portion of the globe where voids created by political weakness and barbarism exist. Sympathy cannot be allowed for ever to block human advancement. In the contest between the higher and the lower order of things, it is impossible to adjust the details to our liking. There is always an intermediate period of partial injustice and confusion before the solution is reached. China can prove no exception to this view. Railroads will eventually appear in the highways of China in place of the ancient and worn-out methods of transportation which now prevail; manufacturing and mining pursuits will be established, her fields will be opened, cultivated, and enriched by modern methods and implements of agriculture. It will be in vain for the Chinese to undertake to support their religion and methods of thought and life by appeals to Confucius and other teachers. These must give way under the influence of modern progress. Why? Because they have produced no fruit. A tree that bears nothing is valueless. China's ethics, laws, religion, and philosophy are barren. Primitively and simply beautiful they may be, but they are without practical value except as historical monuments marking the advance of nations. Her present condition attests the value of her institutions: "By their fruits ye shall know them."

In face of all these facts, it is hard to realise that the allied powers should precipitately have left China. Yet the reason is plain. England and the United States each had a war upon its hands. The Chinese difficulty happened at a most inopportune time, and when the United States inaugurated and persisted in a movement of abandonment of China, England was reluctantly forced to give up her convictions and to join in the retrograde march. Had England been entirely free to act, no doubt she would have forced a different settlement. The McKinley administration exhibited a natural weakness in its policy. It had to fight shy of the imperialistic cry, which had been dinned in its ears *ad nauseam* with respect to the Philippine possessions; it feared another broadside from opposition newspapers, which was imminent if it pursued a strong policy in China, and hence one was hit upon of apparent magnanimity towards the Chinese, but which was at once superficial, weak, and misleading, and withal the worst measure for China which could be imagined. The allied powers entered China without a studied or concerted plan, and they left it without a clear solution or settlement of the questions involved. Their going in was as their coming out—hasty, ill-conceived, and impolitic. The commencement and the conclusion were both befogged. No sooner were the allied troops removed than internal dissensions appeared, and the weakness, wretchedness, and incompetence of the Chinese government was soon more plainly revealed than ever. By abandoning China, the United States played directly into the hands of Russia. England and Germany must have seen this, but they could not combat a plan of action which seemed on its face so magnanimous to a fallen people, especially with France co-operating with Russia.

The whole business must be gone over again. The weakness of China will soon be revealed in plots and revolutions all over the Empire; indignities will be again perpetrated upon foreigners, and armed intervention will follow.

I cannot leave this question without a separate word about France. The *real* position of France should be isolation—waiting, watching, improving. The figure which she presents to-day as an ally of Russia is false and unnatural. Let me speak of France with candour and without reserve. Her national progress is stopped, and an internal decay has set in, which will sooner or later seriously affect her influence as a first-class power. The reasons which impel me to reach this painful conclusion are the following: The effort to establish a republican government in France, while not a failure, is far from being a success. No student who has conscientiously studied the history of the past one hundred years can truthfully say that she has made real progress in government. The attempt to sustain a republic in France has been almost grotesque. The great, central, pivotal point of any serious government is stability, which she has never even approached. Ministries are blown over like card houses, by the mere ebullition of political passion, and not as the result of a principle. The people are genuinely surprised if a ministry lasts six months. In the effort to establish a republic, two great fundamental mistakes—among others—are made. First, the French congress and government are held and administered in Paris, the very centre of boiling passions and the hotbed and school of every conflicting "ism" that arises to confound the good sense and prudence of mankind. The seat of government in a republic must be located away from the cosmopolitan influences of large cities. It must be held in a place where calmness—and quiet prevail, and where the officials of the government, and the legislators, are removed from the intimidating noises and the unhealthy influences of metropolitan journalism.

In the second place, the Cabinet should not participate in the proceedings of the legislative bodies.

A cabinet is chosen to aid the president. As the cabinet members are his family council they ought to be in sympathy with his political views, and with his plans, as executive, and their tenure should be consistent with his pleasure. To place them in a position similar to the Ministry of England, in which nation the House of

Commons represents the immediate sentiments of the English people; to take one important feature of a constitutional monarchy as it exists in England, and place it in the body of a republic like that created in France, is anomalous and incongruous; utterly out of sympathy and in discord with the real purposes of a republic.

In a republic, a cabinet represents the president, not the *people*. The noise, froth, and confusion which characterise every overthrow of a French ministry in the Chamber of Deputies is not the *vox populi*; the change is the result of coalitions, sentiment, or passion; it is a momentary variation in the temper of the legislators, often brought about by events so trivial that one is almost ashamed of legislative bodies. These topsy-turvy movements are not aimed at the executive, but are demonstrations against the cabinet, whose constant overthrow shows the instability of the administration and brings it into contempt. The frequent downfall of a cabinet weakens the confidence of the people in their government, although in fact it may be purely superficial.

I cannot pursue the subject in detail. I leave much unsaid that is important, but there are one or two more thoughts which press upon me with force, and which still further illustrate the above views. France seems to be lacking the few great men who could turn her course into better roads of national policy and prosperity. She has no real leaders. Nor is the nation united in its sympathies with a republican government. That form has no great, genuine lovers in France. They love their country, but not the political mantle which envelops it. Her leading men doubt whether it is the best form for the government of her people, or whether she should not be a monarchy. Democracies thrive upon the love and enthusiasm of the people. If these feelings are not present among the masses, the government is not likely to be healthy. A fair proportion of Frenchmen are socialists. What this means in France, no one has intelligently defined or explained. So far as we can judge from a study of the mass of stuff presented, called argument, it means a general breaking up of society. Another class of Frenchmen favour a monarchy; but perhaps the largest class is composed of true republicans. These differences are vital and fundamental. They go to the form and substance of government, not to its policy, as in America, where every party cry, radical or conservative, is attuned to the music of a republican federation, and which is the *sine qua non* to all political conclusions. How can a nation progress until its people have chosen, or are competent to choose, a stable form of government, and are satisfied with certain organic political principles?

Nothing illustrates the vacillation of France and her utter want of stability more than her alliance with Russia. The extent and nature of this alliance is now known to be of a comprehensive character—offensive and defensive. After France was released from the last obligation of the Prussian war by the payment of the money indemnity, it became the fixed, resolute, and unswerving purpose of her people to regain Alsace and Lorraine from the Germans. Her recuperative power was wonderful. In a few years she was in the full vigour of a new national life. The defeat which the nation had suffered rankled in the bosoms of her people, and for years they thought of nothing but revenge against Germany. The truth is that the result of the Franco-Prussian war casts no reflection upon the moral or physical courage of the French. The fault was that of Napoleon III: the nation was taken unawares, and before she was ready, Germany had her brave people by the throat. The victorious Germans took good care to strengthen their hold on territories wrested from France, by forming the Triple Alliance. In the meantime, the former provinces of France have become in a great measure Germanised. The longings of the people of Alsace and Lorraine to again become part of France grow weaker every day, as do the feelings of the French people to possess them. Separation and time are both acting to diminish the chances of their recovery. On the one side the inhabitants of the territories are becoming acclimated to their new national life; and on the other, the French people have become less intense in their original determination to recover them. A new generation of people has grown up which did not participate in the original struggle, and which lack the enthusiasm of the original actors. Whether French diplomacy could have avoided or thwarted this result, or whether the situation has come from natural or uncontrollable conditions; upon either assumption, the cold, disagreeable fact stares the French people in the face, and they should look at the situation boldly and philosophically—the recovery of these provinces is now a remote possibility.

For years after the Prussian war, France was without an external policy. She knew not where to turn—to the right or left. She glanced with longing, scanning eyes over Europe, and could not select a friend, associate, or ally. She would make no overtures to her historic and falsely assumed national enemy—England; and Germany, Austria, and Italy were tightly closed against her. Russia presented the only open door to her, and after a long courtship she entered into a political matrimony with that great power. A union more unnatural, more lacking in harmony, more ill-advised, could not be imagined. It was a great step for Russia. She could use France admirably in the event of European trouble. French money, and a French army and navy, would make a powerful addition to her own military and naval resources. But what can France possibly gain from such an alliance? Has anyone sufficient ingenuity to plan a campaign by Russia against any power of Europe which would produce an eventual benefit to France? Make up any combination you please and the result would be sure loss to France. Her true policy was to rest where she was—isolated and independent,—quietly abiding the time when the Triple Alliance would be dissolved, or other European complications might enable her to resume control over her lost territories, if ever that were possible. If not, her policy was peace—peace with the world. The alliance with Russia, in advance of conditions which actually demanded or justified it, in form at least, arraigns all Europe against her, and it does her no possible good. The alliance with Russia is meaningless and fruitless. If it has any effect, it is hurtful. The two nations are as far apart as the poles. Point out the incident and page of history where a similar union has been beneficial. It shows a decline in France's external policy, in her prudence and good judgment. It reflects the influences of a weak and declining internal condition. France has forgotten Bonaparte's solemn, almost pathetic appeal to his nation—"Make friends with England." The cultivation of an enmity for England is France's curse. There should be a complete revulsion of national feeling in favour of England—the centre and the source of civilisation. A true friendship with her could not fail to benefit France.

The overwhelming pride of the French, however, hides from them her real internal and external condition. Her only national policy should be peace with all the powers of the world. She should strive to become a purely commercial nation, augmenting the attractions of French life to draw into her bosom the travellers and wealth of the world, and seek, by energy and skill, to retain undiminished her commercial strength against the powerful advances of the Americans.

France refuses to see or admit that since she has lost Alsace and Lorraine much of her national prestige has gone, and while still powerful in many ways, she is destined to second and support, not to lead. Doubtless her people dearly love their country, but they are indifferent to her institutions. They love La belle France, but have no sympathy with her political government. As their great writer, De Tocqueville, says in another connection, they worship the statue, but forget what it signifies. The French are brave and adventurous, — under the inspiration of a great military or naval hero, they will go to the extreme bounds of the earth in search of glory, — but they will not immigrate or travel to found new colonies or foreign homes. If a band of adventurous Frenchmen were to start to-morrow on such a voyage, would it be earnestly coupled with the desire to propagate the gospel of French republicanism? Half of the army and the navy do not believe in republicanism: They would be a sorry set of teachers to propagate the principles of democracy among the natives of a new country. Expansion and imperialism died with the great Napoleon. To-day France is substantially sustained and held together by a species of militarism. The great army moves like a machine to the wishes of each temporary administration. It eats up the vitals of the people and compels them, at the same time, to enthusiastically support it. The moment France gives birth to a great soldier or sailor, he will capture the army and navy and change the form of government into a monarchy or despotism. Deep love or respect for existing administrations does not prevail. Instead of the civil authority of sheriffs, constables, bailiffs, and policemen, the military power is looked to as the real channel for enforcing the decrees of government. The entire conception and development of the army is contrary to true republican principles.

In conclusion, France linked with Russia means nothing for her. She might, with such an alliance, inflict serious damage on England or Germany separately; but it would avail her naught. She should speedily retire from the coalition. Remaining isolated and independent, she can uphold her present prestige, and through the mistakes of other nations she may add to her territorial area, providing she maintains a stable government.

The thoughts, wishes, and energies of her statesmen should be turned to the serious problem of making her people free, prosperous, and happy; as a beginning towards which, let them turn their attention to the eradication of the crying sin of France, the seed that is ripening for her destruction — that evil which Matthew Arnold calls "the worship of the goddess Aselgeia" otherwise "Lubricity."

A final word. Remember, ye Anglo-Saxons, that despite her present condition, France is still, by reason of her large internal resources and enormous wealth, her trained army and modernly equipped navy, a great power in the world, and casting her sword into the scale of events with one or more nations, she can become an instrument of great good or evil. Friendship with her should be cultivated, and her people should be made to see that co-operation with you in your honourable efforts to help mankind is the true line of her policy.

V.—THE SPANISH AND PORTUGUESE PEOPLE

The Spanish-speaking peoples, including the Portuguese, to-day occupy or control 7,918,821 square miles of the territory of the world, exclusive of 1,197,672 square miles in Spanish-African islands, Portuguese Africa and Asia and the Philippines, which would make a total of 9,116,493 square miles.

Their language is spoken in Europe, North, South, and Central America, and in Cuba and Puerto Rico, by more than 80,000,000 of people, which, added to the number of occupants of Spanish African-islands, Portuguese Africa, Asia and the Philippines, would bring the total who speak the Spanish and Portuguese languages in excess of 97,000,000. The statistics are as follows:

	Population	Square Miles
Spain	17,550,216	196,173
Portugal	5,428,659	36,038
	22,978.875	232,211
Mexico	13,570,545	767,316
Guatemala	1,574,340	46,774
Salvador	915,512	7,228
Honduras	420,000	42,658
Nicaragua	420,000	51,660
Costa Rica	309,683	19,985
	17,210,080	935,621
Cuba	1,600,000	41,655
Puerto Rico	953,243	3,600
	19,763,323	980,876
Colombia	4,600,000	331,420
Venezuela	2,444,816	566,159
Brazil	18,000,000	3,218,130
Paruguay	600,000	145,000
Uruguay	840,725	72,112
Argentine Republic	4,800,000	1,095,013
Chili	3,110,085	256,860

Bolivia	2,500,000	472,000
Peru	3,000,000	405,040
Equador	1,300,000	144,000
	41,195,626	6,705,734
Spanish Africa	437,000	203,767
Spanish Islands	127,172	1,957
Portuguese Africa	5,416,000	841,025
Portuguese Asia	847,503	7,923
Philippines	6,961,339	143,000
	13,789,014	1,197,672

RÉSUMÉ.

	Population	Square Miles
In Europe	22,978,875	232,211
In North America and Central America	17,210,080	935,621
In Cuba and Puerto Rico	2,553,243	45,255
In South America	41,195,626	6,705,734
	83,937,824	7,918,821
In Spanish Africa and Islands, Portuguese Africa and Asia and Philippines	13,789,014	1,197,672
	97,726,838	9,116,493[3]

What is the destiny of this numerous race? What relation do its people hold to present and future international problems? What influence will it have in the solution of these questions? As long as the Spanish-speaking peoples remain scattered and without a common purpose in view, its numbers will avail little in the solution of the problems of this century. To be effective, the Spanish and Portuguese people must act together— as a whole.

Now, the striking feature of this race, to-day, is an absolute want of political unity. It has no common and ultimate aim; in fact, all its purposes seem to be discordant and inharmonious. In numbers, the Spanish and Portuguese people exceed the population of Germany and France combined, but their moral influence, in an international sense, is imperceptible. Anything like a real, determined attempt to unite them has never been made. In a word, they are disintegrated, without unity of thought, action, or association.

I find it difficult, in discussing this subject, to separate my feelings from my

---

[3]   The World Almanac and Encyclopedia, 1903. p. 353.

judgment. Sentiment, and some national pride (for I am half Portuguese), struggle hard to impel me to paint a glowing and radiant picture of the future of this race; but the cold, hard facts of history confront me at every step, and it is idle to attempt to distort or juggle with them. If we are to judge the future by the present, the chances of the Spanish and Portuguese people participating in the control of the world are not the brightest. It seems but yesterday that Spain and Portugal owned the greater part of the earth, and were its dominating powers. By huge areas, their territory has vanished from their possession and control until to-day Portugal hardly attracts international attention, while Spain finds her dominion almost shrunken to the proportions of her European peninsular territory and plays a subordinate role in continental politics. I know of no sadder picture in modern history. Let any one turn for a moment to European literature of the sixteenth and seventeenth centuries, for the evidence of their preponderance. In all international affairs Spain in particular is everywhere seen as the first of powers. Her greatness, and the fear it created, seem to start from every page. I cannot pause to go into the causes of this or of the circumstances that favoured it; they are well known. What have we since seen? Her possessions, rights, and powers have been wantonly squandered — simply thrown away, as a result of policies and acts which are utterly irreconcilable with rational principles of true government.[4]

It is impossible not to admire and sympathise with the individuals who comprise the Spanish and Portuguese people. They are noble, warm, generous, brave, and honourable. Like the Anglo-Saxons, they have been hardy rovers and adventurous colonists. The discovery and exploration of new and unknown fields have always been positive and prominent features of Spanish and Portuguese ambition; and yet, when they have acquired territories, they seem to have been utterly deficient in the capacity of holding and uniting them into a great and permanent empire. Individually, they possess all the qualities which excite admiration and respect; aggregately, they seem to lack those elements which so strongly typify the Anglo-Saxon people, whose glory and solidarity now completely overshadow them. God forbid that I should make this statement in a spirit of vainglory or boasting: I am merely recalling what is patent to all who read history, even blindly. A comparison of the two peoples shows that the dismemberment and decline of the Spanish has been in an inverse ratio to the progress of the Anglo-Saxons. As the one sank in the scale of national prosperity, the other correspondingly rose in strength and glory; and in candour it must be added, the latter largely at the expense of the former.[5]

Although physically disunited and scattered, and with no definite, combined purpose of action, in numbers and individual character the Spaniards and Portuguese are still a great people. If they can be brought together they will be factors of the highest importance. Can they, at this stage of their history, cultivate a quality

[4] See in this connection an interesting article by Henry Charles Lea, entitled "The Decadence of Spain," *Atlantic Monthly*, July, 1898.

[5] In 1801, 20.9 per cent. of the people who spoke the European languages were Spanish, and only 12.7 per cent. were English; but in 1890 the ratio was changed to 13.9 per cent. Spanish and 27 per cent. English.

which they have hitherto lacked—cohesiveness?

The age of territorial discoveries seems almost finished. New fields, or new countries, are few. Everything that is to be found has been laid bare to the eyes of the world, and the telegraph gives us hourly pictures of the detailed life of the remotest nations of the earth. With the exception of the poles and the celestial bodies, the occupation of the explorer is almost gone, and the diplomatists and publicists now turn their eyes inward to a study of the possibilities of a division, or separation, of present territorial ownership. The method of acquiring title by occupancy can no longer be exercised, for want of new territory; and the other methods of acquisition—*i.e.*, cession and conquest—now remain the sole means of geographical aggrandisement. With no new fields to explore, the scenes and events of history must be laid in old places, and the diplomatic or political issues will be directed to reapportioning, or redistributing, the old territories.

What part of this great international drama will be assigned to the Spanish and Portuguese people? Can they dominate; or will they be subordinate to one or more powers, and become absorbed in the national life of the latter? Can there be a unification of the Spanish and Portuguese people? Can they cure their present political imperfections? Can they make a thorough introspection of their condition, and follow the proper remedies which it suggests? Can they turn their faces towards the common goal of a free government? Is there a Moses among them, who can lead this great people from the wilderness of political, moral, and financial confusion into the broad plain of a free, enlightened, and modern government?

I shall not undertake categorically to answer any of these questions, but I shall briefly try to lay bare the general existing conditions of the Spanish countries, from which proper and fair deduction may be made. This study may enable us correctly to determine—first, whether the Spaniards can unite; and second, if united, whether they have the capacity to form a permanent, federation, in time to anticipate the march and progress of other nations, whose policy must be to absorb the weaker races in their own political bodies.

I begin with Spain proper. In almost all the essentials of a prosperous government, Spain is, at the present time, deficient. Her treasury is depleted, and financial aid from the outside world practically cut off, or obtainable only upon terms humiliating or prohibitive.

Her army and navy are disorganised. The sources of wealth and employment of the people are shrunken, and in some instances absolutely gone.

Worse than all the above grave difficulties, her people are disaffected with the government, thus giving countenance, on the one hand, to open revolt against it by the advocates of republicanism, and encouragement to the efforts and diplomacy of the Carlists, on the other. Apart from this view, a determined opposition to clericalism prevails, the success of which means actual separation of State and Church, so long and unhealthfully entwined in the operations and administration of the Spanish government.

It will require a clear judgment and a skilful hand to extricate the nation from all these entanglements. But I believe it can be done, and that a wise and firm ruler can guide Spain into a state of prosperity and internal peace, by the introduction of radical reforms in her administration—reforms which will demonstrate to her people that they are abreast with and enjoy the blessings of the freest form of modern government. Whether the boy-monarch who now governs Spain will be such a guide, I cannot predict. But I believe that that country can thrive better as a monarchy, conservatively administered, than as a republic. That the people have felt the impulse existing in all modern societies towards a government of laws combined with freedom, we are assured by recent observers. As is natural, much blindness and indirection has hitherto attended their efforts, but the spirit of the people, though overlaid, survives, and along with it, a strong principle of fidelity and sense of duty, making the best material out of which to build institutions. These, with their noble and hitherto almost impregnable territory, securing them in large measure from foreign interference, constitute what may be called the capital of their natural resources, moral and national. Drawn within herself, self-depending, a new period of substantial greatness may yet arise. Her patriotic fervour has other aliment than the mere recollections of a never well-ascertained or well-founded empire. She can recall that her race has never been subjugated; that it defied for ages the power of the Romans and the Saracens, and that Napoleon at the height of his power failed utterly in the attempt.

If, however, owing to the weakness or inability of the present King to sustain a monarchy, a republic must be tried by the people; if one political experiment after another is to be added to those of the past before a stable and satisfactory government, of some kind, is inaugurated and established, the influence of Spain, during such formative periods, as a party to any consolidation or solidification of the Spanish people, will be dissipated and become merely formal. She can and will contribute nothing substantial to such a movement.

Moreover, if a monarchy is permanently continued in Spain and in Portugal, the hereditary tendency and disposition will be against a federation of all the Spanish people, because federation eventually means republicanism; and it is not natural to believe that the families, in whose hands the monarchical titles are now lodged, can be convinced that the good of the whole Spanish and Portuguese people demands the relinquishment and abandonment of their kingly titles and possessions. Monarchs are sometimes forced to yield up their thrones, or are driven therefrom, by the people; but the spectacle of a king voluntarily surrendering his title for the benefit of his subjects is a rare one. Besides, the indications are that the Spanish people are at heart monarchical. France and her unsatisfactory example may, as a determining cause, have much to do with this tendency.

And in this instance the monarchs of Spain and Portugal can point with considerable force to South and Central America to show that the effort to establish republics among their branch of the Latin race has not been thus far satisfactory, or at least, successful.

But another party whose assent is essential to establish a federation of the whole Spanish people is the United States of America. What are her interests in the premises? What will she say to the formation of a government of this kind, in which two of the leading spirits would be European monarchies, *i.e.*, Spain and

Portugal? What application would be made of the "Monroe Doctrine" to such a condition? I conclude, therefore, that neither Spain nor Portugal would or could be an influential factor in the consolidation of the people speaking their languages.

Can such a federation be established between the republics of South and Central America and Mexico? This would be a government which could start with a population of about 58,500,000 and 7,600,000 square miles of territory.

A common cause and a common necessity drove the thirteen original American States together. But no such force is operating upon the republics of Central, and South America; and they failed to utilise the opportunities presented to them in the past. They are all, more or less, suffering from internal dissensions, and the precariousness of their republican governments is not calculated to impress independent observers with their efficacy, strength, or permanency; yet these republics have no common enemy in Europe or in this country. In fact, from the former, if one existed, they would be protected by the well-settled policy of the United States. Is the United States likely, in any just sense, to become their enemy—an enemy, not of the people, but of the form and method of administering their government? Will not such a condition soon exist in some, or all, of these republics, as will justify and make intervention necessary, on the part of the United States, as was made in Cuba? Could such a possibility drive these republics into a federation, to anticipate what their leaders might term "a coming danger"?

Common jealousies and internal disorders will for some time keep the South American republics from consolidation; but the people of the United States are coming closer and closer, each year, to all of these Spanish republics, and will sooner or later, unless avoided by delicate diplomacy, become actively interested in the affairs of their governments. At that time either one of two things will ensue: the formation of a Latin American federation; or gradual annexation to the United States. As a preliminary to either, or to any, event, would it not be wisdom in this country to tender these republics absolute freedom of commercial intercourse?

And how does Mexico stand? At present she occupies a peculiar and wholly anomalous position. Although in form a republic, Mexico is in fact a despotism. She is ruled by one man, whose authority is unlimited. President Diaz is the absolute and only power in the Mexican government. In theory he holds his title from the people, but his will is omnipotent. And withal, the thirteen millions of Mexicans who make up the population of the different states of the so-called Mexican republic are well governed: thus lending confirmation to the statement, often made, that a despotism, when the despot is a patriot and a wise and pure man, is the best form of government that can be established. As long as President Diaz lives, Mexico will probably continue to be well governed, because her ruler is competent in every sense—honest, capable, strong; and ambitious only to behold his country develop and prosper. But when he dies, what will ensue? Not the regime of another patriotic despot. They do not come in succession, and they do not have political heirs. "God makes not two Rienzis." Diaz's death will reveal to the Mexican people—what they seem, notwithstanding their theories, never clearly to have appreciated—that they live under a republic which gives them the control of all political power. When this period arrives, how many Mexicans will be found capable of exercising the functions of citizenship intelligently and patriotically? Will not a majority of them be dupes or tools in the hands of designing political leaders? Who can assume to rule as Diaz? Whom do they know but Diaz? Is not the population of Mexico inferior, in general intelligence and in the duties of citizenship, to that of any other South American republic? What of the Mexican Indians? How far have they been instructed in the duties of government? What kind of a candidate would they favour? And what will be the outlook for the people under an administration elected by popular vote? I shall attempt to answer all these questions together. The mass of the Mexican people have had no preliminary training for true republican citizenship and government. Diaz's death will produce revolution,—peaceable or armed,—and it will occasion such trouble and turbulence, along the border lines of their territories, that it will become the duty of the United States to preserve order thereon. The interior of Mexico will be thrown into confusion, and the conservative people of the Mexican republic will, in due course of time, appeal to and demand aid from the American republic, as the Cubans did; they will ask for protection, or perhaps annexation. This will not transpire over-night, but it will be the inevitable outcome of history.

The difficulties in the way of consolidation of the Spanish and Portuguese people, therefore, seem to me to be insurmountable. A necessary party to any such federation of a part or all of them is the United States of America; and her consent probably could never be obtained. She is the great, dominating, absorbing power, of the North and South American continents. Her policy must be freedom, equality, and protection to all. She will invade no territories, nor deprive any people, against their will, of the government under which they live. What comes into her family from Mexico will fall into her possession as a ripe apple drops into the lap of earth, naturally, and because the period of complete fruition has arrived.

I have endeavoured to sketch frankly, though briefly, the conditions of the Spanish people and the relation which the United States bears to them, especially to those of this continent. I may be in advance of political thought and judgment—I may have attempted to reveal too much of the future horizon to suit the tardy progress of political calculations. But in considering great international questions, frankness and broad views are necessary. The future is generally of more importance than the present. A policy of patching up or mending existing conditions is always misleading and dangerous. This was seen in our treatment of the Chinese question. We are already experiencing it in relation to Cuba. We started out with a high-sounding proclamation of our intentions, which overlooked, or ignored, the true and permanent interests of the people of that island. "Fourth. That the United States hereby disclaims any disposition or intention to exercise sovereignty, jurisdiction, or control over said island, except for the pacification thereof, and asserts its determination, when that is accomplished, to leave the government and control of the island to its people."[6] Our hands ought to be free to act as circumstances should disclose or dictate. We are now, or soon shall be, confronted with conditions in Cuba which will require us to retreat from our lofty premises and to violate our own declaration. It is a crying evil that in the treatment of great public

[6] Act of Congress, April 20, 1898.

questions our statesmen will not act with openness and frankness, but constantly seek refuge behind false or hypocritical explanations, or use subterfuges to conceal their real thoughts and purposes. It was perfectly manifest that without a preliminary or probative period, the Cubans would not be in any condition to govern themselves, and that an experiment of the present kind must end in misfortune to these people. To put the tools or implements of a free government in their hands and turn them loose to experiment among themselves was an act of folly on our part, and dissipated the advantages gained by independence.

But one word more, apropos of the whole question of the relations of the Anglo-Saxon race to the Russians, Chinese, Spaniards, and Portuguese. Considered either separately or as a whole, they furnish a subject of supreme interest and importance to our people. To me they alone are sufficient and a full cause for a prompt understanding between us. United and acting sympathetically, we can more or less shape the events of the future by a wise and truly beneficent policy. If the English and American statesmen do not agree with me, but leave this question to fate, as it were, there may come storms, cross-currents, deflections, and all manner of unforeseen opposing forces, which will render the unification of our people impossible or futile. Perhaps this is our destiny—but I think not.[7]

And be it clearly understood that in all I have said, I merely indicate what I believe to be the inevitable drift of things—the handwriting upon the wall. With the public morality and the intermediate questions of international law depending on that morality, I am not at present concerned. It is impossible to regulate these questions in advance, and it is assuredly true that such considerations, however well grounded, have never long delayed a general tendency. History, in all its stages, conjectural, traditional, and authentic, discloses with almost painful clearness that there are underlying forces governing the progress of the human race, which are made manifest in successive ages only by their results, and with which conscious volition seems to have but little to do. We in this country only exemplify a general truth (a truth easily ascertainable by a glance at our circumstances), which operates none the less strongly because with our cultivated sentiments we sometimes rebel against its necessary sequences. The only question for me is, how can this truth be best applied—how best utilised. If I am right in what I have said of the Anglo-Saxon race in its two great branches, the inference becomes clear. To that race primarily belongs in a preponderating degree the future of mankind, because it has proved its title to its guardianship. But it is in the firm union of that race, in its steady co-operation, and in its undeviating adherence to its common ideals, that the whole success of the experiment, or of what remains of the experiment, now depends.

---

[7] In this connection I call attention again to the article of Hon. David Mills, Canadian Minister of Justice (heretofore quoted from, ante, p. 13), *North American Review*, June, 1898: "The interests of the world call for Anglo-Saxon alliance. Let not the British Empire and the United States revive, after the lapse of centuries, the old contest of Judah and Ephraim; but, remembering that their interests are one, as the race is one, let them stand together, to maintain the ascendency which they will hold as long as Providence fits them to lead; which will be as long as, in their dealings with those beneath them, they are actuated by principles of justice and truth."

CHAPTER II

THE ORIGIN AND FORM OF THE SUGGESTED ALLIANCE BETWEEN ENGLAND AND THE UNITED STATES

I.—HOW THE SUGGESTION AROSE

Out of the conditions and events to which I have first alluded there arose what I call a desultory, scattered, but emphatic, sentiment among many English-Americans for a closer union, a feeling that a permanent relation of some kind should be established between the United States and the British Empire. There is a prevailing opinion that our race should be more sympathetic, that we should live closer together, know each other better, and think and act in unison on great questions affecting our mutual progress and welfare; in other words, that we should interfuse in our thoughts, acts, and exterior policy. This sentiment for union came upon us suddenly and unexpectedly; it was natural and spontaneous. It was not the creation of man's ingenuity; it was not the invention of diplomacy; it was an evolution. A continuity of a chain of organisms, extending from the lowest to the highest, is an evolution. *"Tous les ages sont enchaînés par une suite de causes et d'effets que lient l'état du monde à tous ceux qui l'ont précédé."* [8]

The existing feeling among the people calling for a nearer and closer relationship of the English-speaking race is the recognition of this evolution.

The belief that steps should be taken to put this feeling into some practicable and tangible shape does not emanate from one country, but it comes from both. It springs not from official or diplomatic sources; it is the spontaneous utterance of the people of both countries.

The peculiar, isolated fact which brought this question to light, and to the attention of the two nations, was the Spanish-American War. The *moral* support which England gave to America in that struggle caused it to develop, and brought about its further propagation. England's position in that war was not manifested in any official or recognised diplomatic manner, but, by some kind of language, intimation, or action known and understood in the courts of Europe, the continental powers were made to understand that she would permit no interference with the United States in the conduct of the war.

---

[8] Second Discours en Sorbonne in *Œuvres de Turgot*, vol. ii., p. 52. Quoted in Buckle's *History of Civilisation in England*, vol. i, p. 597.

Spain also had her friends. At least two great continental powers sympathised with her in the struggle she was making against such enormous odds, and the current belief is that if England's position in this war had not been well known, those powers, with others in the sphere of their attraction, would have manifested their sympathy for Spain in a substantial and combined way. In short, the United States would have had to oppose a European combination. It is not claimed that any such combination was actually formed. The prevailing feeling was that one would have been formed if England's sentiments had not been fully known and declared. Whether this be so or not is now immaterial. I am simply tracing the history of the movement. I am describing the situation as it then appeared.

I find, therefore, that it was a natural condition of affairs which spontaneously brought to the surface this thought of an alliance between England and the United States. In the course of events, the situation of England and the United States, standing *vis-à-vis* to all, or several, of the continental powers, was a strong possibility, and it set the English-speaking races seriously thinking about their fate under such circumstances. The political and military horoscope of Europe was laid bare to them, and they were confronted, for the first time in their history, with the possibility of a war in which they might find themselves in armed opposition to two, or more, or all, of the continental powers of Europe. In truth, many urgent and earnest appeals were, and are, constantly made, in desultory newspaper articles, and in various unofficial ways, in favour of a coalition of the continental powers of Europe against what is termed the "Anglo-Saxon race." The usual arguments are used and the usual epithets applied. They are accused, as race attributes, of "greed," "rapacity," "brutality," and, what is worse, of "hypocrisy." Engaged, as we of the United States were at that period, in a war which we believed to be righteous, we were for the first time in a position to estimate at their proper value such accusations when applied to England herself, and how far they might be considered as the product of senseless fear and blind jealousy and envy.

Before the Spanish War began, no one seriously thought of, or considered, an alliance. It is true that the reading classes among us generally found that in proportion as their knowledge extended beyond one or two given points, their respect and admiration for England became increasingly great. But in practice it was always with some difficulty that the ordinary affairs of national intercourse and business could be adjusted between her and the United States. Like members of the same family, we became easily excited, and were always ready, under such circumstances, to say disagreeable, intemperate, and biting things of each other.

England's covert support and open sympathy with the United States changed our feelings towards the mother country; it awakened our gratitude, and aroused European fear and envy. When Manila was captured by Dewey a new scene in international history was unfolded. The event revealed to the full gaze of astonished Europe the tremendous power and influence of the British Empire and the United States acting in concert.

While there was no actual compact or treaty between the English and Americans, the diplomats of Europe were quick to imagine one. A spectre is always more alarming, and often more effective, than a reality. The situation of affairs was the same as if a treaty had actually existed. The friction, the misunderstandings, the fretfulness, which theretofore existed between the United States and England, and which the other powers of Europe relied upon as a sufficient barrier to prevent any concerted policy between them, suddenly disappeared, and they stood before the world as friends and allies. Here was a new and undreamed-of combination. The cards of diplomacy must be reshuffled, and in future deals the strong possibility of the Anglo-Saxon race being found together, solidly unified, must be considered and provided against.

It should be remembered, that the support given to the Americans, in the Spanish War, was not merely formal, although not sanctioned by treaty. It subjected England to the risk of being involved in serious complications with the other nations of Europe. She took all the risk and responsibility of allowing an impression to prevail that her sympathy, and support, if need be, were with the United States. All the moral force of an actual treaty resulted to the United States from the situation. The position of England, in fact, was precisely the same as if she had openly avowed herself as, and contracted to become, an ally of the United States, and the Americans distinctively gained by it. This episode cannot now be lightly brushed aside. It should never be forgotten by the American people. It was a generous act on the part of the British nation openly to tender its sympathy to the United States. It was voluntary and unsolicited. England did not stop to discuss and analyse the causes of the war with Spain. She placed herself by our side on the broad grounds familiar to her own people, and gave us full credit for the rectitude of our intentions, as proclaimed by ourselves.

There was no qualification attached to her sympathy. It would have been an easy task for casuists and international lawyers to have raised an argument in favour of Spain, but it was not heard in England. There were no public meetings in the British Empire to protest against our war with Spain: none of her orators, or well-known public men, or high officials, denounced our conduct as unjustifiable or unrighteous. Not a word of that kind was heard from any respectable quarter. There was never an occasion in history when national gratitude was more justly due from one nation to another. The less we say as to how this debt has been repaid the better our feelings and manners. We must, *at least*, candidly admit that many American criticisms of England in the Boer War have been in a very different spirit—sufficiently ill-bred, harsh, and unfriendly. That may be passed by. Difference of opinion on such subjects is natural, and language is generally exaggerated in proportion to ignorance of the subject. But a more recently developed sentiment among us is deserving of severer censure: a few of our people are disposed to turn the sympathy and assistance of England at that critical moment into a ground of complaint against her; not only is her friendship denied and denounced, but she is accused of having beguiled us into the paths of imperialism, and our rulers share in the denunciation, as having succumbed to her blandishments—a monstrous and wholly unique instance of political perversity.

It must not be assumed, however, that a feeling of gratitude, on the part of the United States, should be manifested or repaid by making an alliance with England. This would be mere sentiment,—commendable but misplaced. An alliance based upon such a foundation would be built upon quicksand. Gratitude is a noble quality, but it is more dangerous than gunpowder when applied to political affinities.

But to return to the main subject; the *thought* of an alliance between the English-speaking people grew out of the Spanish-American War, and speculations, at first limited to a purely military view, of an offensive and defensive treaty between the two nations, for temporary purposes, have gradually grown and enlarged, until they have led to conjecture concerning the whole future of the English-speaking nations, their wealth and resources, their religious, moral, and political growth and destiny: they have also led to researches into the history of the past; thus embracing both a backward and forward view.

Happily, the thought of an alliance has sunk deeply into the minds of many serious people, who realise that in a seemingly accidental, certainly unpremeditated, way, a great historical truth has been uncovered, which, in its full growth and maturity, may lead to the greatest epoch in the history of the English-speaking race. The Spanish-American War, lamentable as it was in some of its aspects, inevitable in others, surprising in all, may hereafter be regarded as an event of supreme importance in the history of England and the United States, just as the accidental discovery of the *Corpus Juris Civilis* was to the world of that period, in enabling it to form new conceptions of law, and through these conceptions to advance many steps in its progress from barbarism to civilisation; or, to bring the illustration closer home to us, as the accidental assembling of a few enterprising men in a London inn gave rise to the undertaking of Sir Humphrey Gilbert, and that, in its indirect results, to the enormous possibilities inherent in the fact of the establishment of the Anglo-Saxon race on this continent.

II.—THE INDEFINITENESS OF THE FORM OF THE PRO-POSED ALLIANCE

Although much has already been said and written upon this great subject in the United States and England, the suggestions respecting closer relationship have been most general and indefinite; and, with a single exception,[9] so far as I can discover, no one has ventured to outline a plan by which a tangible result can be reached. It is agreed that a "better feeling," a "better understanding," a "better knowledge" of each other, a "closer union," more "intimate relations," an "*entente*," should exist between the people of the two countries.

But what is meant by these terms, or, when defined, how to carry them into practical effect, is left in total darkness. It is impossible to make any real progress in the discussion of the question, unless some accurate landmarks are made; a starting-point must be fixed, from which arguments I may proceed, and upon which conclusions may be established.

To an intelligent discussion of any subject, a definition is a *sine qua non*. What is meant by "alliance," "union," a "better understanding," a "closer relationship," "interfusion," an "*entente*," and terms of like import? It is in vain that the citizens

---

[9] See article of Professor Dicey, *The Contemporary Review Advertiser*, April, 1897, p. 212, recommending the establishment of a common citizenship.

of both countries may *wish* or *hope* for a better understanding, or that a better feeling, or a closer relation, or union, should exist between them. It is said that idle wishes are the most idle of all idle things.

In what does closer relationship consist? And how shall it be brought about and cemented? What is the thing to be accomplished? What are the reasons for its accomplishment? And by what methods can it be accomplished? These are the salient inquiries.

In search of light upon this question, I have taken as a basis of discussion a resolution adopted by the "Anglo-American League," a society formed in London in the summer of 1898, consisting of representative individuals, chosen from all grades of social, political, civil, and commercial life, which was as follows[10]:

"I. Considering that the peoples of the British Empire and of the United States of America are closely allied in blood, inherit the same literature and laws, hold the same principles of self-government, recognise the same ideals of freedom and humanity in the guidance of their national policy, and are drawn together by strong common interests in many parts of the world, this meeting is of the opinion that *every effort should be made, in the interest of civilisation and peace, to secure the most cordial and constant co-operation between the two nations.*"

Here is a clear and well-defined presentation of the subject: first, the _postulate, i.e., _the people of the two countries are closely allied in blood, inherit the same literature and laws, hold the same principles of self-government, recognise the same ideals of freedom and humanity in the guidance of their national policy, and are drawn together by strong common interests in many parts of the world; second, the _motive, i.e., _in the interest of civilisation and peace; third, the _conclusion, i.e., _every effort should be made to secure the most cordial and constant co-operation.

This resolution crystallises the combined thought of all the orators and writers who have contributed to this subject; and furnishes a clear text for a full discussion of the whole question. The facts contained in the resolution, that we are "closely allied in blood, inherit the same literature and laws, hold the same principles of self-government, recognise the same ideals of freedom and humanity, . . . and are drawn together by strong common interests in many parts of the world," are sufficiently serious to justify and support the conclusion that "every effort should be made . . . to secure the most cordial and constant co-operation between the two nations," — especially as the high and noble motive which impels this effort is "in the interest of civilisation and peace." Here is a "motive and a cue" which should enlist, not the Anglo-Saxon race alone, but the sympathy of the whole Christian world.

But how, when, and by whom are such "efforts" to be made, to secure this "most cordial and constant co-operation between the two nations "? The resolution, speeches and articles referred to give little or no light on these important

---

[10] The Chairman of this League was the Rt. Hon. Jas. Bryce, M.P.; the Hon. Treasurer, Duke of Sutherland; the Hon.Secretaries, T. Lee Roberts, Esq., R. C. Maxwell, Esq. LL.D., Sir Fred. Pollock, Bart.

points. No plan is laid down; no ways or means suggested by which objects so highly extolled and so important, shall be accomplished. The public men of both countries advocate an *entente*, a "cultivation of better relations" between the two peoples. They shudder at the mere suggestion of a written treaty or executed alliance. In these respects their advice and acts are conservative. But is it safe to leave the subject in this indefinite condition? Should we not advance another step or two in the direction of a real national fraternity? The question should not be allowed to remain in this doubtful and unsatisfactory state. The noble purposes of this resolution cannot be attained by *mere words*. *Acts* must follow the *wishes* and *declarations*. Every assertion of this resolution should be clearly and explicitly proven; the objects to be accomplished by co-operation demonstrated; and the plans by which they shall be carried into effect determined, and, if practicable, enforced.

At present we have advanced no farther in the question than this: It appears that many persons on both sides of the Atlantic have a wish, a feeling, a sentiment, a belief, a conviction, that it is for the mutual benefit of the British Empire and the United States that co-operation, interfusion, union, should be permanently established between the two countries.

This is the first step in the movement. Discussion, argument, controversy, properly precede acts. A spirit of scepticism, as Buckle says,[11] certainly a spirit of inquiry, must arise previous to actual steps being made in any great movement. But, if the statements contained in this resolution are correct, it is the duty of every citizen of England and the United States, in fact, the duty of citizens of all countries, to commence the agitation of the question; to bend their energies to its solution, and to aid in the quick and complete consummation of co-operation. If the purpose of co-operation is to secure "civilisation and peace" to the inhabitants of the world, it is not merely the business of Englishmen and Americans to see that it succeeds, but it is a matter in which all mankind is interested. The question is not limited to those of the English-speaking family; it is as broad as humanity itself.

No reason has been assigned why the consummation of this important subject should be postponed or evaded. On the contrary, existing conditions require that it should be pushed to a solution. It has come to stay—to be solved. Great events cannot be ripped, untimely, from the womb of history. They are born at regular periods of political gestation, and when thus ushered into the world, become ripe for discussion and action. They cannot be smothered. They must be met and settled. Of course, the professional politicians, especially those of the United States, will not touch this great subject of "union." They will await events. They will gauge its popularity. They will study its effect and influence upon the Irish and German vote. They will play with it until it becomes a burning, absorbing, national topic, and when the wind of popular approval blows that way, they will outrival each other in its advocacy. The politicians are born for the hour. A learned, thoughtful, and dispassionate advocacy of any public question, by a professional politician, would be a *rara avis* in national life. The inherent strength, reason, and justice of great public questions, are never considered by these nimble gentlemen—in fact, perhaps they never were. The business of politics involves only the present.

[11] Vol. ii., *History of Civilisation*, etc., p. 1, note.

The motto of the politicians is "Policy," "Expediency"; not "Truth," "Reason," and "Stability." In the primitive stages of this discussion, therefore, it is left in the hands of the independent, non-partisan thinkers. This class must mould it into tangible, practical shape, before it can be brought into the realm of ordinary politics.

III.—DEFINITION OF CO-OPERATION, ALLIANCE, UNION, OR COMPACT

Our first aim, therefore, is to discover what kind of co-operation should be established between the two nations. And this may be accomplished by stating what is *not* meant to be included in the term.

I take it that the sincere advocates of co-operation, union, interfusion, do not mean, by these or kindred terms, an "offensive and defensive" treaty, or alliance, between the United States and the British Empire, for the mere temporary purpose of commercial or material aggrandisement, or conquest, or for military or naval aggression, or defence. If that be the scope and limit of this movement, it might as well be dropped, as utterly and wholly impracticable. In fact, an offensive and defensive treaty, in its common acceptation, has already been discarded by the advocates of union. The great end and purpose of the resolution, to "secure civilisation and peace," cannot be attained by such means. To ascertain the source from which co-operation and interfusion between the English-speaking people arises, to distinguish Anglo-Saxon union from other forms of international alliance, it seems a necessary prelude to the discussion of the subject to recall the primary ends of government. In whatever form it exists, its ends may all be summed up in the idea of benefit, or advantage. It is so in the most arbitrary despotism that ever existed among men; it is so in the most enlightened free system; the difference being that through progressive development in the several succeeding conditions of society, the free government confers greater benefit and advantage. We need not now consider the former; we have to do with the latter only. As it is, in the modern sense, its *raison d'etre* is the harmonious blending of all classes of society; the preservation of the essential interests, wisely understood, of the people; the preservation of an open field for the exercise of every virtue and every talent, and, subject to these, the performance of every duty enjoined by good neighbourhood, and the encouragement of every tendency and impulse which points to the amelioration of mankind, at home or abroad. Such is the idea of a commonwealth, constructed on true, liberal principles, and sanctified by Christianity.

As an individual is endowed with intellectual, moral, and physical functions for the purpose of ennobling his own existence, benefiting his fellow-men, and reaching by these means a higher plane of moral and religious life, so government, as we now understand it, is organised to place it within the power of men to enjoy to their fullest extent, religious, civil, and political liberty; or, to express it in another way, to give an individual those rights, privileges, and liberties which the true and purest thoughts of the past ages have determined as the best rule for his real happiness.

The peculiar and striking characteristic, or virtue, of the Anglo-Saxon people is, that they understand the objects for which governments are instituted more directly, and apply them more successfully and broadly than other peoples. They keep more closely in view the origin and aim of political society in its relation to individuals, and to other nations—to the world at large. Montesquieu frankly made this admission in 1748, when he said: "They know better than any other people upon earth how to value at the same time those three great advantages, *religion, commerce,* and *liberty.*"[12] And Mommsen made the same admission when, with evident reference to the English race, he said, it knows how to combine "a love of freedom with a veneration for authority."

And Mr. Webster uttered the same thought:

"I find at work everywhere, on both sides of the Atlantic, under various forms and degrees of restrictions on the one hand, and under various degrees of motive and stimulus, on the other hand, in these branches of a common race, the great principle *of the freedom of human thought, and the respectability of individual character.* I find, everywhere, an elevation of the character of man as man, an elevation of the individual as a component part of society. I find everywhere a rebuke of the idea, that the many are made for the few, or that government is anything but an *agency* of mankind. And I do not care beneath what zone, frozen, temperate, or torrid; I care not what complexion, white or brown; I care not under what circumstances of climate or cultivation, if I can find a race of men on an inhabitable spot of Earth whose general sentiment it is, and whose general feeling it is, that government is made for man—man as a religious, moral, and social being—and not man for government—there I know, I shall find prosperity and happiness."[13]

In the foregoing we have the motive and justification for a combination of the Anglo-Saxon people.

The words "to advance civilisation" have been very frequently used in the discussion of this topic as a motive for alliance or relationship. This word "civilisation" is an easy word to invoke to cover false policies, and is often flippantly applied without a real idea of its scope. It is important therefore, to have a clear understanding of its meaning. It means, primarily, *to reclaim from a savage or semibarbarous state.* This, then, presents the first step in the efforts of a nation—I may say its first duty—to those within and without the fold of its sovereignty—to reclaim mankind from a barbarous and savage state. The conquests of savage tribes and nations have been many times justified upon this broad principle; such historical events as the conquest of America and of British India can perhaps only be supported on these grounds. The attainment and diffusion of civilisation is not accomplished without much suffering and loss, but this is as natural as the growth of a plant from the seed. Pain and suffering are the inevitable concomitants of birth and growth. Man is ushered into the world through the travail of his mother, and the birth of civilisation is not excepted from the rule which applies to particular individuals.

---

[12] *Spirit of Laws,* vol. ii., p. 6.

[13] From speech delivered on the 22nd of December, 1843, at New England Society of New York, on the Landing of Pilgrims at Plymouth, Webster's *Works,* vol. ii., p. 214.

To *introduce order and civic organisation* among those reclaimed from a savage or barbarous state is the secondary meaning of the term "civilise." Order is a necessary element in the formation and development of society. To understand and apportion among men their respective positions in society; to define all the rights and duties of individuals and put them in their proper places, is the great aim of government; and as order is "Heaven's first law," so it is the corner-stone of human association. As nothing is more pleasing and striking to the human eye than a well-regulated and orderly household, everything in its place, clean, refined, and harmonious, so nothing is so necessary to a good government as simple, proper, well-defined, orderly rules of conduct for its citizens. A nation which invades and conquers a savage tribe, or uncivilised nation, and in place of the chaos, confusion, and at times unspeakable cruelties which there prevail, introduces order, civic government, and humanity, is creditably fulfilling its ambition and national purposes.

In the noble words of Cicero "nothing earthly is more acceptable to that first and omnipotent God who rules the universe, than those Councils and assemblages of men (duly ordered) which are called States."

But following the reign of law, the profound significance of which I will not now pause to dwell on, there is a third meaning attached to "civilise": it means to *refine* and *enlighten; elevation in social* and *individual* life. In the second and third meanings of this term, we have the guarantees of liberty, justice, equality, fraternity. After the first step, therefore, of conquest, reclaiming people from a semi-barbarous or savage state, there comes the second state of civilisation,—order and civic government,—followed by the third degree,—refinement and enlightenment, elevation in social and individual life. These different stages of national growth are all illustrated in the progress of civilisation.

Now, the history of the English-speaking race shows a constant advance from a semi-barbarous state to a high degree of civilisation. It has never gone backwards in its march from one degree of civilisation to another. At times, it is true, it has been diverted; at other times, generally from the pressure of external causes, it has apparently paused, and it has seemed as if its mission were at an end; but it soon resumed the forward movement, until to-day it leads the van of civilisation; *i.e.*, barbarism has disappeared to give way to order and civic government, and refinement and enlightenment pervade, create, and elevate social and individual life. One can trace the progress of the English nation as plainly as the growth and development of a human being; from weak, puerile infancy into strong and sturdy manhood; suffering all the diseases that flesh is heir to, but eventually overcoming them, and advancing with renewed vigour and health in the march of its destiny.

I mean no offence to other nations—all modern European governments have shared in a general way in the same movement; all may have their specific excellences, but we know our own best, and are justified in thinking that it is more indigenous, better built and better founded, follows surer methods, and is more conspicuously entitled to gain the applause and fulfil the expectations of mankind.

I therefore lay it down as a basis of an alliance, or union, that the British. Empire and the United States mean, in all sincerity and good faith, when they establish co-operation, to work for civilisation and peace; to move harmoniously and sympathetically together for the accomplishment of this great object—namely, the benefit of mankind. This, then, is the central, true, deep, absorbing purpose of their alliance, an interfusion of ideas, principles, sympathies and thoughts of the people of both countries; acting, working together, and co-operating to accomplish a common purpose, mission, and end. We must mingle together in thought, and in sentiment; we must be allies in the noblest sense of the word; not friends merely in aggressive and selfish enterprises, but locked together in a common thought and common purpose to achieve the great and glorious object of civilisation. And let this purpose be broadly, clearly, and comprehensively stated, in some declaration, *in some writing, perpetuating the compact of union—let us write a second Magna Charta, or a second Declaration of Independence; commemorate our joint purpose in some imperishable instrument, upon which may be written declarations so clear and convincing that the world can never mistake our purposes or misconstrue our motives.*

CHAPTER III

THE HISTORICAL FACTS TRACED WHICH HAVE BEEN GRADUALLY LEADING TO INTERFUSION BETWEEN THE ENGLISH-SPEAKING PEOPLE

ARE we the chosen race of Israel? Are we the peoples of the earth, elected to lead the van of civilisation and peace?

Let our competency and integrity of purpose be judged by our present lives, by our civilisation and government, and by our past history. When we discuss the ability, competency, and fitness of an individual for a public or private trust, we begin by examining into his character, his mental and intellectual acquirements, his business capacity; his experience, his past life and conduct. We gauge and weigh every element of his moral and intellectual nature, and our judgment is formed by the results, good or bad, which flow from the examination.

Now, a state or government has a character precisely like an individual. To analyse it, understand and appreciate it, we must search the records of history; we must examine and weigh every important epoch of its national life to determine its fitness, its trustworthiness, and its ability to be charged with the great mission of civilisation and peace. We must sum up its influence upon its own people, as well as consider the effect of its national life and character upon other nations.

Before I proceed, then, to examine into the motives and reasons which operate on the English and American nations to justify a union, it is well to inquire into their national character. In the light of history, how do the Anglo-Saxon people stand? Guided by such, how should the outside world estimate us? Is the compact we are contemplating a false or unholy one? Is it for the present and future inter-est of the English-speaking people to make it? Will this union militate against the interests of the other nations of the world?

I do not propose to attempt to recall the history of England—not even in the briefest form. I will simply bring to notice certain salient epochs, which I will use as monuments to mark the progress of the Anglo-Saxon race, as it journeyed from its primitive, formative condition to a state of enlightenment. I do not stop to dwell upon intermediate history, or attempt to explain, palliate, or justify acts which of themselves may seem to deviate from the general character of the people. Such acts, indeed, were part of the conditions of their growth. I take my readers to a high vantage-ground, and point out to them the long pilgrimage of the nation from its untutored infancy to the shrine of its full manhood. And I shall hereafter consider the subtle, all-pervading influences which their institutions, laws, language, and literature have had upon the formation of national and individual character.

I.—THE DIFFERENT EPOCHS WHICH LED TO THE DEVELOPMENT AND EXPANSION OF THE ENGLISH-SPEAKING RACE

(a) The Introduction Of Christianity Into England

The English race began its outward and more apparent national life as a band of marauders, rovers, and pirates, by chasing, in a large measure, the original Celtic inhabitants of Britain from their soil, and taking possession of it. The exact motives which induced them to make these excursions to that island, or the circumstances which surrounded them, are lost in the darkness of the past. Probably they were prompted by mere rapacity and the gratification of the spirit of enterprise. The tribes which are now distinctly marked, as the Engle, Saxon, and Jute, belonged to the same Low German branch of the Teutonic family, and were, as it is said by the historians, at the moment when history discovers them, *being drawn together by the ties of a common blood, common speech, common social and political institutions*. There is perhaps no ground for believing that these three tribes looked on themselves as one people, or that they adopted the name of Englishmen when they first settled in England, but each of them was destined to share in the conquest of that island, and it was from the *union of all of them, when its conquest was complete, that the English people has sprung.*[14]

The real national life of the people, however, commenced in the sixth century, when Gregory (597) sent the Roman abbot Augustine, at the head of a band of monks, to preach the Gospel to them; and, as among the Greeks, the religious tie thus created, became the strongest tie.

The flood of new thoughts and new purposes which Christ had opened to the Eastern world began, by this time, to permeate Europe. The distinctive features of Christ's precepts and life, considering Him as a pure teacher alone, were that He instructed men how to make the best use of their mental, physical, and spiritual faculties. Consequently, as individual character is the real basis of human society, Christianity became a necessary part of government. At first, it was a plant of slow growth in English soil, but the seed, once sown, took firm hold, and to-day, in England, North America, and in the colonies of the British Empire, Christianity, avowedly or essentially, is strongly and healthfully entwined in all its constitutions and governments, — a strong principle of cohesion, yet yielding to the people an unrestrained freedom of religious opinion and worship of the most unqualified character.

Of course, I do not overlook the immense benefits of Christianity common to all the nations among which it was introduced; it made the great distinction between ancient and modern civilization—between ancient and modern life. But, in England, it was so far peculiar, that its ready and peaceful acceptance, and the

---

[14] Green's *History of the English People*, vol. i., pp. 7-8.

purposes of political homogeneity to which it was turned, indicate a distinct national characteristic. All the subsequent religious history of the country, even after diversities arose, bears evidence of the same general truth. In the contests through which society sought its amelioration, we can discover always that "intimate connection between personal liberty and the rights of conscience and the development of public liberty so peculiar to the English race."[15]

I take the introduction of Christianity into England to be the *first great step* in her natural and national progress—the first span in the bridge which led from barbarity to civilisation. Its influence upon the people can be profitably studied in the typical Englishman, King Alfred.[16]

Of Liberty, the poet Shelley sings with equal truth and beauty:

> "And then the shadow of thy coming fell
> On Saxon Alfred's olive-cinctured brow."

We have recently celebrated the millennium of this illustrious ruler. It should be made an occasion for the advancement of the purposes I am here opening. These purposes would have been Alfred's.

(b) The Consolidation Of The Different Kingdoms Of England Into One

Although from the time of the landing of the Jutes, Saxons, and Engles (449), their history is jejune and scanty, and the occurrences of four centuries have been condensed by an accomplished historian[17] into a few pages of history, yet sufficient appears to show that the several governments established by them in England were engaged in many bloody and bitter intestine contests, and that the consolidation of the people was first effected by Egbert (about 827). This union lasted only five years, and we are told that it was brought about, "for the moment, by the sword of Egbert." It was a union of sheer force, which broke down at the first blow of the sea robbers—the Northmen—who, about this time, invaded England. But the very chance which destroyed the new England was destined to bring it back again, and to breathe into it a life which made its union real. *"The peoples who had so long looked on each other as enemies found themselves confronted by a common foe. They were thrown together by a common danger, and the need of a common defence. Their common faith grew into a national bond, as religion struggled, hand in hand, with England itself, against the heathen of the North."*[18] They recognised a common king, as a common struggle changed Alfred and his sons from mere leaders of West Saxons into leaders of all Englishmen in their fight with the stranger, and when the work <u>which Alfred set</u> his house to do was done; when the yoke of the Northmen was

[15] See Article on "William Penn," by Theodore McFadden, in the *Magazine of the Pennsylvania Historical Society*, for December, 1883.

[16] "England felt the full heat of the Christianity which permeated Europe and drew, like the chemistry of fire, a firm line between barbarism and culture. The power of the religious sentiment put an end to human sacrifices, checked appetite, inspired the crusades, inspired resistance to tyrants, inspired self-respect, founded liberty, created the religious architecture, inspired the English Bible."—Emerson's *English Traits*, p. 164.

[17] Green's *History of the English People*, vol. i., p. 89.

[18] *Ibid.*, p. 90.

lifted from the last of his conquests, Engle, Saxon, Northumbrian, and Mercian, spent with the battle for a common freedom and a common country, knew themselves, in the hour of their deliverance, as an English people.[19]

The work of Alfred was to save the Saxon name and existence—that he accomplished. His conquest, on the other hand, was never complete. His wars ended in compromise, the Danes retaining large settlements in the North and East of England. Subsequently, their invasions were renewed. In Canute's reign, they were the prevailing people. In all these life-and-death struggles, there is nothing that detracts. The Danes should be considered as a cognate people, alternating with the Saxons, and finally blending with them; quite as often defenders of the soil as invaders, and contributing largely to the formation of the national character. In the struggle against the Norman king, they were the last to succumb.

The union which each several tribe within the nation had in turn failed to bring about was realised from the pressure of the Northmen. It seems that at the close of the eighth century, the drift of the English people towards national unity was utterly arrested. The work of Northumbria had been foiled by the resistance of Mercia; the effort of Mercia had broken down before the resistance of Wessex; and a threefold division had stamped itself upon the land. So completely was the balance of power between the three realms which parted it, that no subjection of one to the other seemed likely to fuse the English tribes into an English people; yet the consolidation of the several kingdoms of England into one was eventually reached.[20]

It was the *second step* in its national progress.

What brought it about? Mark this well. The instinct of self-preservation, of which the ambition, more or less enlightened, of the several petty kings, was the instrument; the external force in the ravages of the Northmen; the marriages and alliances between the tribes; in fine, all of the same causes which to-day are operating with greater force towards the unification of the English-speaking peoples.

Compare England in this connection with the Grecian cities. The unhappy destiny of the latter was complete before they realised the benefit of consolidation, and when it was at last advocated, and in some small degree adopted, it was too late. We read of the Ætolian League and the Achaian League, but only as studies to the political thinker of an idea to which there was always wanting the power of fulfilment. Where lies the difference? Not in intellect, surely, for no race has ever surpassed the Greek in intellect. In what then? Simply, as I understand, in *character*—in that especial endowment by which the Anglo-Saxon race so moulds itself, in its civic and social relations, as to attain the highest purposes of political wisdom, moderation, the subordination of self, the rejection of false or impossible ideals, together with a kind of innate perception of the value of time and occasion, in combination with persistency, stability, and courage—these are the qualities which have made its institutions at once models for the rest of the world, and the subjects of its envy. The fatal disease of small political entities ran through all the

[19] Green's *History of the English People*, vol. i., p. 90.
[20] Green's *History of the English People*, vol. i., p. 90.

Grecian states, and they were doomed. Consolidation, with the Greeks, was never more than a faintly formed idea; with the English, like all other political conceptions, it soon became a fact.

(c) The Influence Of The Roman Law Upon England's Progress

A civilising influence of the highest importance was the absorption of the Roman law into their legal, ecclesiastical, and political systems. It is an epoch in the progress of the English, which, although impossible to say at what precise period its influence was the greatest upon their people, I call the *third* span in the bridge from an immature to a civilised state.

It is certain that the Romans had establishments in England from the time of Claudius (A.D. 43) until the year A.D. 448. During the greater part of these four centuries they governed it as a Roman province in the enjoyment of peace and the cultivation of arts. The Roman laws were administered as the laws of that country, and at one time under the prefecture of their distinguished ornament, Papinian.[21]

To estimate its influence upon the progress and development of England, one must be prepared to accept the now generally recognised opinion, that the Roman Law permeated every branch of jurisprudence—property, procedure, criminal law—all. It was ubiquitous, and even the feudal system, whose origin was attributed, by most of the common-law writers, to the time of William the Conqueror, is shown to have existed long anterior to that reign; and was, probably, the creation of the Romans.

The jurisprudence of Rome was, and has ever been, an unfailing fountain, whence the English people have drawn copious draughts of wisdom and knowledge.

I do not mean by these observations to detract from the common law—crude as it may have been as a science—for, in all that relates to the principles and protection of civil liberty, it was infinitely in advance of the Roman Law.

As a political system, the Roman Law was framed to be the instrument of the despotism, under which it was perfected. As in everything else, the English Law reflected the political genius of the people. They extracted and preserved the good, and rejected the evils, of the Roman system, the absorption of which exhibits keen power of assimilation.

(d) The Great Charters; The Petition Of Right; The Habeas Corpus Act, Passed Under Charles, The Bill Of Rights In 1688, And The Act Of Settlement

The Great Charter of King John contained very few new grants, but, as Sir Edward Coke observes, was mainly *declaratory of the fundamental laws of England.*

But from his reign (1199) until the end of the reign of William III. (1700), a period of almost exactly five hundred years, the English nation was engaged in enlarging, deepening, and strengthening the forms of a constitutional monarchy. Thus, the Great Charter was confirmed in Parliament by Henry III., the son of John. In

---

[21] Reeves, *History of the English Law*, Finlason, vol. i., p. 161.

the next reign of Edward I., by statute called *confirmatio cartarum*, the Great Charter was directed to be allowed as the common law. And by a multitude of statutes between the last-named reign and that of Henry IV., its principles were again declared and corroborated. Hume enumerates these statutes as being thirty in all.

Then, after a long interval, and much backward and forward movement, thrillingly interesting to the student, came the parliamentary declaration of the liberties of the people, assented to by Charles I., in the beginning of his reign, and celebrated as the Petition of Right. Subsequently, the Habeas Corpus Act was passed in the reign of Charles II. To the above succeeded the Bill of Rights, delivered by the Lords and Commons to the Prince and Princess of Orange in 1688. Lastly, the liberties of the people were again asserted at the commencement of the eighteenth century in the Act of Settlement, whereby some new provisions were added for the better securing of religion, laws, and liberties, which the Statute declares to be "the birthright of the people of England," according to the ancient doctrine of the common law.[22]

I take this great struggle for laws and liberty as marking another distinct and remarkable epoch in the history of England—the *fourth* span in the bridge of her growth and development.

I am travelling rapidly through the ages of English history; but not going so fast as not to be able to see that the nation and her people are constantly progressing.

(e) The Union With Scotland

The *fifth* great epoch in the History of England, is the union with Scotland; by which the Kingdoms of England and Scotland, on the 1st day of May, 1707, became united as one under the name of Great Britain. The Act which created this union did not constitute between the two nations a *federal alliance*, but an "incorporated union," the effect of which was that the two contracting states, in their dual condition relatively to each other were totally annihilated, and they became, thereafter, one political entity, without any power of revival.

It is not essential to trace the history, anterior and subsequent, which bears upon this great event; yet we may profitably reflect, that, arising out of centuries of hostility and mutual injury, here also were the most inveterate prejudices to be overcome, upon the one hand; on the other, partial similarity of race, language, and institutions, and, in the view of statesmen, the most *enormous advantages*. Under wise and skilful management, the latter were at last made to prevail. It is, however, notorious, such was the perverse opposition, particularly in Scotland, the nation most to be benefited, that notwithstanding the preparation for the event by a long train of antecedent causes, had the measure been referred to a plebiscitum, it could not have been carried. Can we now do other than smile at such wilful blindness, such well-intentioned folly? It is a most interesting page in history, and in the present connection it carries with it the force of an authority.

(f) Discovery Of America

----

[22] Blackstone's *Com.*, vol. i., p. 128 *et seq.*

I now turn to another epoch closely connected with the progress of the English-American people.

In the fifteen centuries which followed the birth of Christ, many important and profoundly serious historical events are chronicled, but the sublimest fact of them all, after the introduction of Christianity, is the discovery of America. The intelligence, ambition, courage, influence, and progress of the English race are nowhere more strongly illustrated than in the events which follow this portentous event: it constitutes the *sixth* great epoch in the history of the English-speaking people. Originally controlled by the Spanish and French, this great North American Continent, little by little, but by sure and regular steps, at length came completely under the domination of the Anglo-Saxon race. I do not dwell upon this epoch as a mere spectacle of military and material conquest. I point to the great results which have flowed from it. Every acre of ground they acquired, either by conquest or purchase, they have retained, planting in its soil deep and indestructibly the seeds of their policy, religion, and government. No revolution, no time, no partial infusion of other races, has been able to eradicate the English-American principles from the ground in which they were originally sown.

There is a marked and impressive similarity between the conquest of Britain by the Engles, Saxons, and Jutes, subsequently consolidated into England, and the conquest or absorption of the North American Continent by the English-American people. The original Britons, as such, have almost entirely disappeared. And where are the aborigines of North America? A few bands of Indians constitute the vestige of the race which peopled the North American continent when the hand and power of the Anglo-Saxon people were laid upon it. Pause and reflect upon this conquest: how it was accomplished; the principles which justified the invasion of the country, and the acquisition of the territory of the Indians. It was not merely greed and conquest that actuated the settlers. Granted that they were not always above the ordinary motives which actuate humanity, still in the main, it was the spirit of discovery, the inextinguishable thirst for enterprise, so marked a characteristic of the race, which impelled them. And, as we so well know, these qualities were often combined with the noblest motives;—the desire of finding absolute freedom for their religious opinions and worship, which the necessities of the political situation at home denied them. Go back to the aim and purpose of government for a justification of these acts, preliminary to the introduction of order and civic government in the midst of a savage and barbarous country. Behold the introduction of English principles, laws, literature, into the great North American continent. While with heartfelt sympathy we deplore the sufferings and extinction of the earlier possessors of the soil, do we not clearly see that it affords a conspicuous instance of that Providence which shapes our ends, rough hew them how we will?

(g) The Independence Of The Colonies

The *seventh* great epoch in the progress of the English-speaking people, conceiving them as a whole in their growth and expansion, is the separation of the colonies from the mother country and the establishment of the Republic of the United

States. It constitutes one of the most important links in the chain of circumstances which makes up the history of this people. It is perhaps the greatest expansion of a kindred race that history has ever recorded. It has been accompanied by such a fecundity of population; such marvellous personal and aggregate wealth; such phenomenal development of individual and national prosperity; such wonders of science, art, mechanical invention, and commercial greatness; such enormous discoveries of mineral treasures; such superabundance of agricultural resources, as to amaze the very faculties of eyes and ears. Yet it is said by some persons, because of the revolution of 1776, that this phenomenal offspring of England, whose similarity of speech, laws, literature, customs, complexion, manners, in fine, of everything vital, is so striking, should shrink from a closer union with her maternal ancestor; that overtures to push farther their onward march towards civilisation and peace should be treated either with indifference or positive scorn and contempt! And this revolution of 1776, which was in reality but a further expansion and propagation of the English race, and the principles of English liberty, laws, and government, we Americans are advised by a certain class to look upon as a barrier to closer ties between kindred people! This argument is so unnatural, so unchristianlike, so contrary to the laws of human affection; so opposed to our mutual interest and progress; so antagonistic to the good of mankind; so utterly unfounded in reason and history, that I doubt whether it does not fall by its own inherent weakness.

The Revolutionary War, in its outward form, commenced as a struggle for the right of representation, and was afterwards extended to a demand for absolute liberty and independence. But, inherently, it really was the struggle of natural laws in aid of future growth. Although the immediate contest grew out of what was, in effect, an infraction of political rights and liberties, beyond all this were these natural causes operating to produce separation. The peculiar situation of the colonies, the immensity of their possessions, their remoteness from the mother country, the enormous difficulties of intercommunication, produced such isolation in space, notwithstanding much love of the "old home" and pride of ancestry, that an eventual parting between the two countries was simply inevitable.

The War of 1776 was a family quarrel, and bitter, as all family quarrels are. It had been brewing for at least ten years before open war was resorted to, and the history of those ten years, when closely studied, shows that natural conditions were accelerating and encouraging the formal demands which the colonies were to make of the mother country. There is no reason to believe that if the demands had been adjusted, the union of the countries would have been long preserved.

The truth is, that the son had arrived at full, mature age. The maternal mansion was too small for his energy and ambition, and could not accommodate his growing demands and wants. He threw off his allegiance to the mother country, and set up for himself in a separate establishment. It is doubtless true that the maternal rule, by being, in some particulars, narrow, rigid, and unjust, accelerated the eventual demand for that broader national life which was opening in the domains of the new world, and I do not mean to deny that the arguments used by the colonists to justify their separation were not sound. Weaker reasons than those advanced, however, would, as circumstances were, have amply justified the steps they took to establish their independence. The inherent necessities were present, and reasons were easily found to warrant extreme measures. On this side of the Atlantic, in our historical treatment of the subject, we have confined ourselves in the main to the immediate causes and events of the unhappy quarrel, and it is a singular evidence of the candour and conciliatory spirit of the English, that their writers have, in most instances, accepted our version of them, and even enhanced upon them; nay, have even glorified in them as affording another example of the keen-sighted love of liberty inherent in the race.[23] Nothing is more complete than the national self-abnegation (if the expression may be allowed) with which the subject is treated by English authors. Might not we Americans at this time of day, in a spirit of equal fairness, find some apology for our then antagonist? As thus: that the struggle was conceived and precipitated by a handful of infatuated politicians and a narrow-minded King; that the pretext turned upon a point of pure *legality*, such as has always been found to have a tyrannous influence over minds so constituted — a point, however, to which none of our warmest defenders were able to find a legal answer; that at every stage of the question it was contested by an opposition in Parliament composed of men of exalted talent and purity of purpose, whose speeches and writings on the subject are among the most precious gifts of political eloquence and wisdom, and who were willing to sacrifice their own political existence in proof of the sincerity of their advocacy of our cause; that a similar powerful opposition existed in the country, where the name of Pitt was still a charm to conjure by; that if we had been content to wait for a brief time, that opposition must have come into power, and, as in the case of similar reactionary movements in England herself, the broader doctrine must then have prevailed, and every vestige of tyranny, and every cause of disagreement, been swept away. We might ask ourselves whether, being human, we were altogether impeccable! England under the government of Chatham had valiantly come to our aid, and, after a vast expenditure of blood and treasure, secured this continent for her sons; and the subject of the partial reimbursement, in behalf of which she taxed us, was the staggering debt incurred in our defence. There was a measure of truth in this, and narrow and inexpedient as was the attempt at coercion, in the eyes of statesmen, it was just one of those errors into which ordinary mortals are most apt to fall. The quarrel once begun had, of course, the usual tendency to aggravate itself by intemperate speech and action. As to *antecedent conditions*, let comparison be made between English, and French, and Spanish methods of colonial government. In them Mr. Burke, our most ardent and enlightened advocate, could find nothing to condemn. He commends the wisdom of the general system and "the wise neglect" of previous administrations. No one who has read the speech on "Conciliation," can ever forget the magnificent tribute to the rising greatness of the colonies, and to that "Liberty" which we possessed, and which made that greatness. Even the Navigation Laws, ugly blemish as they were, were strictly in accordance with the economic ideas of the time, and as such were introduced and accepted. Compare them, again, in their practical operation, with those of France and Spain. Mr.

---

[23] A recent instance is Sir George Otto Trevelyan's *American Revolution*. Still later, however, is the work of Edmund Smith, *England and America after Independence*, a strong and bold defence of English policy after the separation.

Burke deplores them, but "as our one customer was a very rich man" he remarks that, until a very recent period, they had been scarcely felt as a disadvantage. That seems really to have been so. Franklin, in that inimitable examination before the Committee of the House of Commons, admits as much, and says further, that, in his opinion, those laws would not of themselves justify the resistance of the colonies. Upon the whole subject, in a conversation with Burke, Franklin confessed his fear that the condition of the colonies, in the new order of things, would be less happy and prosperous than in the old. It was about this time that the doctrines of Adam Smith were beginning to take root, and it is certain that in less than half a generation the whole restrictive system, as applied to the colonies, would, notwithstanding the selfish opposition of the mercantile classes, have vanished like a dream. As to the kinds of government bestowed on the colonies, they were mostly of their own choosing, and in advance of the times. Mr. Lecky remarks of them that "it cannot with justice be said that they were not good in themselves, and upon the whole, not well administered." Locke, the friend of all liberal government, gave his genius and virtue to the elaboration of one of them. Penn's model of government was in advance of his times and in the forefront of ours, and it is believed that the Calverts sought to embody the ideal perfections of Sir Thomas Moore's Utopia in the Constitution of Maryland.

The truth is, that but for the natural causes impelling to separation, the whole contention might, and should, have been treated as a domestic one, in which, by virtue of the underlying principles of the British Constitution, all that was wisest and best would have triumphed, and there would have arisen out of it, for both countries, an edifice stronger and more beautiful than any which had gone before it. It was not to be. What remains to us now is the fervent wish that all that was evil in the controversy may for ever perish from the memories of men, and in aid of that wish, the consideration that, as we were the *victors*, to the *victors belongs magnanimity*, especially when the *victory was over our own kith and kin.*

And in this temper of mind we may reflect that the War of the Revolution was to us, in certain vital aspects, unmistakably a blessing—it brought Union and the Constitution. Every student of our history knows how deeply seated were the diversities between the States, and what slight causes might have inflamed them into enduring antagonisms; how embarrassing such conditions were to Washington and the statesmen of the period; how, as a consequence, through what opposing forces the ideas afterwards ripening into the Constitution made their way. The Union and the Constitution, as we have them today, were, then, the direct products of that struggle. Without its impelling influence, it is more than doubtful whether they would have been realised at all. I can recall no instance in history where such peculiar results have been reached, and permanently maintained, where opposing passions existed and have been left to their natural operation. There has been some active countervailing impulse—some determining motive. We had such a motive in that war and reached the result, but even then only after "difficulty and labour huge." More fortunate, or more virtuous than the Grecian communities, after their heroic defence against Persia, we found in our successful resistance the means of security against internal dangers infinitely greater than any external ones, and along with them the opportunities of our highest achievements in the field of political wisdom.

In this capacity for turning to account a situation fraught with immense danger, do we not recognize that *our* ancestors were in accord with *their* ancestors in similar situations? Do we need to be again reminded of the *history* of Magna Charta, of Representation and the House of Commons, of the Petition of Right, and of the English Constitutional System dating from 1688?

One other thought in this connection. The war which broke out in 1754 between France and England, was, in relation to us, a war essentially for the control of North America, and England unfalteringly sustained the colonists in that struggle. If France had been successful in that war, and had established her supremacy in the North American Continent, what would have been the fate of Americans? How long would have been deferred the establishment, by them, of a separate republican government? Would it ever have been established in its present form? The narrow escape the colonists had from the domination of French power can now be clearly seen by those who read the history of that time. The French driven out, there was nothing to counterbalance the drift towards independence.

I am sure that there are few, if any, Englishmen who, however much they may deplore the animosities which have been evoked out of that episode in our common history, would now wish to undo the results of the American Revolution. France looks with envious and covetous eyes upon her ancient provinces, Alsace and Lorraine, wrenched from her by a foreign power, but England regards with pride the development, accomplishments, and wealth of her offspring, and, with genuine regret for the past, turns yearningly towards it.

In thus restoring the subject to its historical integrity, so far from weakening, we strengthen our side of the question. Why should we sacrifice any fraction of the truth when we have so little need to do so? Nakedly, under the circumstances, and free from all legal and metaphysical abstractions for or against, it was plain that the claims of the English Parliament did, practically, involve consequences that we might well regard as fatal to liberty, and, constitutional remedies failing, as justifying an appeal to arms. The conviction of our ancestors that nothing less than this was at stake rightly superseded all other considerations, and was as profound and sincere as similar convictions for similar principles, recorded in the annals of the race. The more clearly we obtain a view of the subject in its simplicity, the less will we be disposed to conceal, exaggerate, or distort its contemporary aspects, either of facts or morals. "It was against the recital of an Act of Parliament, rather than against any suffering under its enactments, that they took up arms. They went to war against a preamble."[24]

And yet we are likely to be told that one of the barriers against any present alliance between the two nations grows out of this Revolutionary War. If that event constitutes no impediment to England, why should it cause embarrassment to the United States? England was defeated and the colonists established their government. Is this event, now shown to be a natural step in the expansion and

---

[24] See Mr. Webster's speech on the Presidential Protest, *Works*, vol. iv., p. 109.

development of the English-speaking people, to be used as an argument against their further progress? If so, why? The English nation does not put forth such a claim. Why should we Americans allow a spirit of hatred or prejudice to grow out of our own triumphs? In a sense England fought for union with us, and if the war of 1776 furnishes any ground against the present establishment of a union of feeling and interest between ourselves and her, how much more forcible would be the argument when applied to the present and future relations of the North and South? The results of that fratricidal struggle, by which the latter people sought to separate from the Union, have been fully acquiesced in. The animosities and prejudices which were engendered by it have disappeared, and the relations of the people of the North and South are solidified by new feelings of deep and sincere friendship, union, interest, and patriotism. The results of that struggle, unhappy, dreadful as it was, have proved to be of profound moral and material benefit to the people of both sections. The results of the Revolution of 1776 have been of like great advantage to both England and the United States. History is full of civil wars, of family quarrels among kindred peoples, in which the result has been, not separation of the parts of the community, but their better integration. Look at England herself; all her internal dissensions grew out of the same principle, which, when established, left the people more firmly united, and on a higher plane than before. Indeed, as all national systems are based upon an association of families, it would be impossible to form any political society if past wars and animosities between them were not forgotten; and the same principle applies to communities homogeneously related, although technically separated. Look again at England and Scotland before and after the union!

The motive and reason for the unification of the English-speaking people is manifest, and certainly nothing is more unsound, nothing is more vain, than to search in the closets of history to find skeletons of past quarrels, battles, hatreds, and conquests, to frighten them away from their true duty and interests.

Examine the history of England before the time when the separate kingdoms into which she was divided were consolidated, and what do we find? Constant and bloody wars between them! And yet, the instant a union was established, and these different people became one, how quickly the old spirit of prejudice and hatred was buried in the grave of the past, and how joyously the people entered upon a new era of progress and national success! Assume that King George and the English Ministry bitterly tried to prevent our independence; take it for granted that England compelled us to go to war with her in 1812; admit that a portion of her people sympathised with (and gave substantial support to) the South in the Rebellion of 1861. What then? Does it follow that these events, buried in the vaults of the past, should be brought out as arguments against the accomplishment of acts clearly for our present interest, conducive, if not necessary, to our future security and peace? The individuals who composed the British Empire when all the above facts transpired, are no more, and the causes which then operated upon them have also long since disappeared. A learned historian has said: "The God of History does not visit the sins of the fathers upon the children."[25] Shall men be

---

[25] Mommsen.

less liberal—less forgiving? Why should we then reject the proffered and sincere friendship of our own kindred? Is it only among nations, and such nations, that "no place is left for repentance, none for pardon"?

England to-day, in respect to the individuals who compose it, is not the England of yesterday. She recognises the independence of the United States as the work of her own offspring; that which she once sought to prevent she now hails as a blessing. The past is buried; a new era is ushered in; new light illumines our purposes, motives, and acts. Through the instrumentality of a closer and quicker communication, we have become better acquainted, our mutual wants and necessities are better understood, the relations of each nation to the other are more clearly defined, and out of all these conditions we can plainly foresee that we have a common purpose and destiny to fulfil—which can only be accomplished by a genuine fusion of the whole people.

Let the words of a poet, which have become a household possession of the English race, be applied in letter and spirit to the situation.

> "I doubt not through the ages one increasing purpose runs,
>
> And the thoughts of men are widening with the process of the Suns.[26]

These truths are happy "prologues to the swelling act of the imperial theme." The sublimest is now before us. The unification of the English-American people in the glorious mission of civilisation and peace is the next great preordained step in their national life. Diplomacy might have laboured in vain to create it; but neither prejudice nor demagogism can now thwart or prevent it. Who will stand forth to challenge or prohibit the banns of such a national matrimony? Let him show cause in the Court of Civilisation why the doctrines of religion, liberty, humanity, and peace should not control the result.

II.—RÉSUMÉ OF THE FOREGOING

I pause a moment to look back upon the ground I have covered—to sum up conclusions. I have endeavoured briefly to point out in the preceding observations the great historical landmarks which have been made by the English-speaking people in their march towards the twentieth century; I have shown the *seven* spans which make up the bridge from their infancy to manhood.

We find them starting life at first as rovers and pirates, crude, unlettered, barbarous; great sailors; great soldiers; indefatigable, full of courage, adventure, and hope. They established separate governments in England, the Jutes here, the Angles there, and the Saxons everywhere. They absorbed into their own free system of common law all the abstract principles and the forms of procedure of the Roman law, which system had had a growth of several centuries in England before the Romans evacuated the island. We behold these tribes adopting Christianity. Then comes union between the kingdoms, with all the benefits which the consolidation of discordant and warring states produces; the growth of commercial power; the encouragement and development of their internal interests; the entry of the people into enlightened national life; the creation of England itself. Then follow

[26] Tennyson—Locksley Hall.

centuries in which the nation at times seemed to go backwards, at other times to stand still, or, again, at others, to leap forward, with, on the whole, a steady social advance, until the consummation of the union between England and Scotland, so long retarded. From that period we behold the people making steady and sure progress in their national life. But long before this last-named event, England had started in the great work of colonisation, in spreading her people over the earth, with the consequent advancement of her commercial interests, and the dissemination of her laws, institutions, language, habits of religious thought, and manners. America was discovered, and she soon claimed and held a commanding position on the American Continent, from which she and her children were never to be dislodged. Then followed the Revolutionary War, and the subsequent establishment of the American Republic—that marvellous political progeny of England. A separate government was created, with English laws, institutions, language, literature—everything.

What is more instructive than the review of the progress of this great race of which I have sketched the outlines, but of which, as I have said, the details are innumerable? Are the Anglo-Saxons to be trusted? Are they worthy of belief when they assert that their purpose in fusion is to secure the establishment of civilisation, and the maintenance of all the best interests of mankind? Are they the proper custodians of liberty and happiness, of "peace and good will"? Do not judge them by any single, isolated fact in their history, but, adapting your views to a philosophical consideration of the subject as a whole, ask yourself, upon your moral responsibility, what other or better guarantee for the attainment of the ends proposed is afforded you than the history of their race.

CHAPTER IV

THE INHERENT NATURAL REASONS OR SYMPA-THETIC CAUSES WHICH SUSTAIN A UNION, AND WHICH SUPPORT THE HISTORICAL GROWTH AND TENDENCY TO THE SAME END EXAMINED

I RECUR again to the resolution of the Anglo-American League:

"Considering that the people of the British Empire and of the United States of America are closely allied in blood, inherit the same literature and laws, hold the same principles of self-government, recognise the same ideals of freedom and humanity in the guidance of their national policy, and are drawn together by strong common interests in many parts of the world, this meeting is of the opinion that every effort should be made in the interest of civilisation and peace to secure the most cordial and constant co-operation between the two nations."

An inquiry into the practicability of forming a more perfect union between the English-speaking people involves the consideration, first, of their *internal* relations; and, second, their *external* relations to the other nations of the world.

What are the motives, influences, and causes which operate to induce the English-speaking nations and colonies to form a closer union than that which now exists between them?

Of what real advantage is interfusion-brotherhood—union?

I shall endeavour to take up the subjects in their natural order:

I.—UNION NATURAL AS TO TIME AND PEOPLE

In the first place, then, the union is a *natural* one, both as to the time of its taking effect, and as to the people embraced in it.

In respect to the *time*: the question of a union has not been forced upon the race or dragged into public light at an unseemly period by the artificial influences of diplomacy or official negotiation. It has come before the people in a perfectly natural way—unexpectedly, and unaccompanied by any strained or superficial influence. It is the inevitable result of primary and natural causes, which have been ripening and developing, noiselessly and slowly, to this end. In a word, it is an evolution.

Passing from the question of time, the union of the Anglo-Saxon people is a *natural* one. It is an alliance of nations of one

> "clime, complexion, and degree,
> Whereto we see in all things nature tends."

It is not a union between nations speaking different languages, possessing different characteristics, laws, sympathies, or religious, moral, or political institutions. It is not a union between the English and Chinese, or the American and Japanese. It is not discordant, grating upon the senses or feelings—unnatural. Nor is it an alliance for temporary purposes and gains, or for purely selfish motives or interests, or for offence or defence. Neither, on the other hand, is it a union of mere sentiment, a dangerous quality except when under the control of reason both in nations and individuals. It is a union which has become necessary in order to fulfil the destiny of the race—it is as natural as marriage between man and woman. It consummates the purposes of the creation of the race.

II.—OF THE SAME NATIONAL FAMILY

What are the different elements which constitute, or make up a natural alliance?

We belong to the same *national family.*

It is true that we do not live in the same land, but are more or less scattered over the world.

It is also true that we do not exist under the same form of political government. We are, nevertheless, one family, descended from the same stock, and attached to each other by the inseparable chain of political, religious, and moral sympathies. We are inspired by the same conceptions of truth, justice, and right. We are living separately, as families live apart who are too great, or too numerous, to exist under the same roof; or who have separated to extend or enlarge their wealth, influence, and power; and we have scattered ourselves over the face of the globe, faithfully carrying with us all the original ideas and sentiments which we imbibed from the mother bosom.

I give first place to this element of family nationality when inquiring into the natural conditions which impel a union between the English-speaking people. England is the mother country; the United States, Canada, Australia, and the other colonies are her legitimate offspring. We are direct descendants of England. We, citizens of the United States, are her greatest and most direct offspring. When we separated from her, we took her language, her laws, her morals, her religion, her literature, with us; in fact, we left nothing of value behind us. In a word, we are so strongly marked with her lineaments, that it is impossible, if we wished, to deny her maternity. No matter whom our remote ancestors were previous thereto, it is certain that since the time of Alfred, we have a direct and uncontrovertible lineage. Our national pedigree from that epoch can be clearly, even vividly traced. But however interesting in other connections, I see no good or profit to be derived from entering into ethnological or philological discussions as to who constituted our direct or remote ancestors, or to spend time in tracing the origin and course of our language. Neither is it worth while to advert to the contention, that there can be no English-American alliance while we have among us so large an infusion of a nondescript foreign element. The same reasoning could have been equally applied to the union between England and Scotland. Such blending gives force to the contention in favour of the mission of the dominant stock race, abroad and at home. The reasons for an alliance do not rest upon a correct or technical decision of these points. It is an undeniable fact, that previous to the reign of William the Conqueror, and for a limited time thereafter, the English nation was composed of heterogeneous elements, and that a great admixture of foreign blood was injected into the veins of her people. In truth, the vigour, character, and virtue of the English nation is largely attributable to the influences which this admixture of outside and alien blood has had upon it. To-day she opens her doors to foreign immigration with fewer restrictions than we do. The nations which have erected a barrier against the outside world, refusing to mix or mingle with strangers and foreigners, have sunk into final decay or ruin. Admixture of blood, within due limits, is an indispensable element to a strong, lasting, vigorous, national life. It is, besides, one of the duties imposed upon the highest civilisation, and necessary to its diffusion.

"The narrow policy of preserving, without any foreign mixture, the pure blood of the ancient citizens, had checked the fortune and hastened the ruin of Athens and Sparta. The aspiring genius of Rome sacrificed vanity to ambition and deemed it more prudent as well as honourable to adopt virtue and merit for her own, wheresoever they were found, among slaves or strangers, enemies or barbarians."[27]

In respect to the United States of America, it has been well and often said that her population is largely made up of foreign elements, and that she is in this respect the most heterogeneous of all nations. The remarkable fact, however, is that this foreign element disappears, almost like magic, in the bosom of American nationality, and assimilates itself almost immediately with the laws, habits, manners, and conditions of the country. The foreigners who have immigrated to this country, and embraced, through the naturalisation laws, American citizenship, have come here, for the most part, to make this their permanent abode. In assuming this citizenship, their foreign prejudices, thoughts, and habits have become absorbed in their new political life and duties. As rain, falling upon banks of sand, leaves no trace of its existence, so these foreigners, swallowed up in the immense and busy life of this country, soon pass unnoticed and undistinguished, into the walks of American citizenship. This great faculty of absorbing and assimilating the heterogeneous and foreign admixture of blood, contributes to the wonderful success of the American Republic. All that remains of the foreigner's country, after he becomes naturalised, is a memory of the past. In one or another harmless form, through social, fraternal, musical, and other societies, he keeps alive the sentiments of his childhood and youth, and reproduces the images of old homes and old friendships. But his new political and social convictions are as fixed and immovable as rocks.

The loyalty of these new citizens to existing republican institutions is fervid and genuine, and once here, there is no effort on their part to introduce or propagate the political habits of thought, or the institutions, of their mother country.

[27] Vol. i., Gibbon's *Roman Empire*, p. 256.

They are not only content with the liberty and political conditions which prevail; but they become the most ardent supporters and advocates of our Democracy. In comparison to the number of immigrants who reach our shores, few of them, as I have said, ever permanently return to their own countries. But notwithstanding the great mass of foreigners who help to make up our population, it is very evident that the predominating element of the country traces its ancestry back to the British Isles; that there is more of her blood in the veins of Americans than that of all other nations combined. Illustrations of the strength of this remark can be found in all the walks of the political, civic, military, naval, religious, scientific, commercial, and literary life, of the people. What is it but another triumph of the race and its civilisation? It is not without interest to trace the ancestry of our Presidents, and of some of our prominent statesmen, military and naval officers, financiers, merchants, writers, and scholars. The latter classes I have picked out at haphazard—without invidious distinction.

PRESIDENTS	
1. GEORGE WASHINGTON…..	English.
2. JOHN ADAMS…………	English.
3. THOMAS JEFFERSON……	English.
4. JAMES MADISON………	English.
5. JAMES MONROE……….	Scotch.
6. JOHN QUINCY ADAMS…..	English.
7. ANDREW JACKSON……..	Irish, of probably Scotch descent.
8. MARTIN VAN BUREN……	Dutch.
9. W. H. HARRISON……..	English.
10. JOHN TYLER………..	English.
11. JAMES K. POLK……..	Irish.
12. ZACHARY TAYLOR…….	English.
13. MILLARD FILLMORE…..	English.
14. FRANKLIN PIERCE……	English.
15. JAMES BUCHANAN…….	Scotch-Irish.
16. ABRAHAM LINCOLN……	English, probably.
17. ANDREW JOHNSON…….	English, probably.
18. U. S. GRANT……….	Scotch.
19. JAMES A. GARFIELD….	English.
20. CHESTER A. ARTHUR….	English.
21. RUTHERFORD B. HAYES..	Scotch.
22. GROVER CLEVELAND…..	English.
23. BENJAMIN HARRISON….	English.

24. WILLIAM McKINLEY…..	Scotch-Irish.
25. THEODORE ROOSEVELT…	Dutch-Irish-Scotch.
STATESMEN	
1. DANIEL WEBSTER……..	English.
2. HENRY CLAY…………	English.
3. JOHN C. CALHOUN…….	Scotch-Irish
4. BENJAMIN FRANKLIN…..	English.
5. SAMUEL ADAMS……….	English.
6. PATRICK HENRY………	Father-Scotch descent. Mother- English descent.
7. JOHN RANDOLPH………	English (some accounts say Scotch).
8. SALMON P. CHASE…….	English.
9. WILLIAM H. SEWARD…..	Father—Welsh descent. Mother—Irish descent.
10. CHARLES SUMNER…….	English.
11. JEFFERSON DAVIS……	Father—Welsh descent. Mother—Scotch-Irish descent.
JURISTS	
1. JOHN MARSHALL………	Welsh.
2. JOHN JAY…………..	Father—French descent.
3. OLIVER ELLSWORTH……	English.
4. JAMES KENT…………	English.
5. JOSEPH STORY……….	English.
6. ROGER BROOKE TANEY….	English.
7. WILLIAM M. EVARTS…..	English.
8. RUFUS CHOATE……….	English.
9. SAMUEL J. TILDEN……	English.
SOLDIERS	
I. NATHANAEL GREENE……	English.
2. WILLIAM TECUMSEH SHERMAN..	English.
3. WINFIELD SCOTT……..	Scotch.
4. PHILIP H. SHERIDAN….	Personal memoirs (autobiography) says parents were born and reared in Ireland.
5. ROBERT EDWARD LEE…..	English.
6. THOMAS JONATHAN JACKSON..	Scotch-Irish. (STONEWALL)
7. JOSEPH E. JOHNSTON….	Scotch.

8. GEORGE HENRY THOMAS…	Father—Welsh descent. Mother—French Huguenot descent.
9. NELSON A. MILES…….	Father—Welsh descent.
SAILORS	
1. EDWARD PREBLE………	English.
2. OLIVER H. PERRY…….	English.
3. ANDREW HULL FOOTE…..	English.
4. WILLIAM BAINBRIDGE….	English.
5. DAVID GLASCOE FARRAGUT..	Father—Spanish descent. Mother—Scotch descent.
6. STEPHEN H. DECATUR….	French descent.
7. RAPHAEL SEMMES……..	French descent.
8. GEORGE DEWEY……….	English descent.
FINANCIERS	
1. ROBERT MORRIS………	English.
2. ALEXANDER HAMILTON….	Scotch descent.
3. ALBERT GALLATIN…….	He was descended from an ancient patrician family of Switzerland.
4. J. PIERPONT MORGAN….	Father—Welsh descent. Mother—English descent.
WRITERS AND SCHOLARS	
1. JAMES RUSSELL LOWELL..	His stock was distinctly of English origin.
2. OLIVER WENDELL HOLMES..	Dutch and Puritan ancestry.
3. EDGAR ALLAN POE……..	From his father he inherited Italian, French, and Irish blood. His mother, Elizabeth Arnold, was purely English.
4. HENRY W. LONGFELLOW….	English descent.
5. RALPH WALDO EMERSON….	English descent.
6. JOHN GREENLEAF WHITTIER..	He was of Quaker and Huguenot descent.
7. WASHINGTON IRVING……	Scotch descent.
8. NATHANIEL HAWTHORNE….	English descent.

III.—THE SAME LANGUAGE

I now come to consider the *third* element which goes to make up the *natural* character of the alliance.

We have the same language. The inhabitants of the United States of America, and of Great Britain, not only speak the same language, but it is their *native* tongue. How can we overrate in this respect the enormous value of a common language — an influence which, according to the use made of it, may be either healing and remedial, unifying and progressive — the source of all that is most beneficial and delightful, or else jarring, discordant, retroactive, and pernicious. Ought it ever to be forgotten that to the mother country belongs the glory of originating and forming this great language?

It is one thing to speak and understand a language; but it is quite a different thing to have inherited it, to have been born with it; or even to have acquired it, as a necessary concomitant and auxiliary to citizenship. One may acquire a language as a traveller, linguist, or as an accomplishment; or from the temporary necessity of office, occupation, or livelihood; but language acquired, for either of these latter purposes, no matter how perfectly, is merely formal and incident to education, and creates no sentiment of country, home, patriotism, or national pride. An Englishman speaking French, or a Frenchman speaking English, has no sympathy with the customs, laws, manners, morals, legends, literature, or drama of the foreign country beyond the acquired one of scholarship. The range, influence, and effect of the native tongue, however, is that of the air. We cannot see it or touch it. We cannot transcribe, or limit, its scope or power. We only know that it was born with us; that it is our constant, ever-present companion. It is with us in our sleep, in our dreams. It is omniscient, and omnipresent. It is a heritage that no time, influence, or condition can take away from us. He who would describe the influence and importance of language upon those who are born with it, must be able to encompass the air which we breathe, and say what are its limits and effects upon human life.

The intercommunication of ideas between people who use the same native tongue is a source of pleasure and joy, of pain and sorrow, of love and hatred. It brings to the surface from the innermost depths of the soul, from the hidden recesses of the mind, the sensations of home and country. It draws from the perennial and inexhaustible fountains of memory, genius, and inspiration the mysterious accumulations of thought harboured there, and sends them floating through the world to distinguish men from beasts. In some languages the same word expresses both speech and reason, and therefore conveys the distinctive idea of man.

The sands of the seashore, the drops of the ocean, are few when compared to the mighty current of words which are poured into the world by millions upon millions of human tongues. It is the tie of a common language which indefinably and inexpressibly knits together all those who have inherited it. "The tie of language is perhaps the strongest and most desirable that can unite mankind."[28] The English language is a synonym of English thought, passion, pleasure, pain, suffering. It expresses all our intimate and fundamental ideas of law, religion and politics. It means home, parents, relatives, and friends. It conveys to the mind all the hopes, wishes, aspirations, and emotions of the English-speaking races.

When an Englishman and an American meet, no matter how casually, their common tongue furnishes, immediately, a means of communication which makes them "Native to the manner born." A few spoken words, a few lines of correspon-

[28] De Tocqueville, *Democracy in America*, p. 33.

dence, open up, if need be, the whole life of each nation: its politics, its forms and principles of justice, its religion, its domestic interests and feelings, its science, its drama, its literature, its past, present, and future. It establishes a sympathy and bond in all common things. If they discuss a question of municipal law, they know without explanation the principles and proceedings applicable to it. If literature, they immediately refer to some common standard. Details are understood and employed without comment or explanation. Their common sympathies, their common methods of thought, their common judgments, are substantially the same. They may differ in form of expression and thought, and in other superficial outward methods, but ideas of the principles of a free constitutional government, of justice, right, truth, liberty, and religion, are cast in the same uniform mould in English and American breasts. If confronted with one of another race, their language in these respects would at once evince their common origin. Despite individual prejudice and personal dislikes, there is a substantial groundwork of sympathy between an American and an Englishman as to what is fundamentally right and wrong, and as to how the right should be asserted and the wrong redressed and punished, even to the minutest degree of assimilation or repugnancy. And this is so, even where there may be a difference of opinion as to the merits of the immediate subject of controversy.

An Englishman and a Frenchman, meeting for the first time, although capable of expressing themselves in one or both languages, have no common ideas or sympathy in questions of law, religion, politics, history, or literature. Such questions, even among cultivated people, are only treated of in the abstract. One word, which would open a fountain of sympathy between Englishmen and Americans when speaking to each other; would be a dry well of thought to a Frenchman, German, or Russian, involving long and intricate explanations, even where there was more than average intelligence and knowledge on both sides. That indefinable and untranslatable perception of English and American manners, customs, and tastes—which, Mr. Burke says, are stronger than laws—can never be conveyed or understood except by the native English tongue, to a native Englishman or American.

It is impossible to enhance the importance of this uniformity of language, in holding the race together and in rendering the genius of its most favoured members available for the civilisation of all.

As Mr. Grote says of the Greeks,[29] "Except in the rarest cases, the divergences of dialect were not such as to prevent every Greek from understanding and being understood by every other Greek." Language, therefore, made in all its widely spread settlements the bond and badge of the Greek race. Without it, other instrumentalities of co-operation, such as religion, would not have been available.

It is due to their common language that all the Greeks come to us as one people; yet Homer was Scian; Anacreon, Teian; Pindar, Bœotian; Sappho and Alcreus, Lesbian; Herodotus, Carian; Aristotle, Stageirean. Language dissolved all differences between them. Notwithstanding the invincible political obstacles which kept them apart, by virtue of language, they all gloried in the name of Hellas, and eagerly disputed who was best entitled to that name, and who had best illustrated

[29] Grote's *Greece*, vol. ii., pp. 319 and 320 *et seq.*

its greatness. A stimulating and fruitful rivalry!

The same thought is elaborated in other relations by Professor Freeman.[30]

"Primarily, I say, as a rule, but a rule subject to exceptions, as a prima facie standard, subject to special reasons to the contrary, we *define the nation by language.* We may at least apply the test negatively. It would be unsafe to rule that all speakers of the same language must have a common nationality; but we may safely say that when there is not community of language there is no common nationality in the highest sense. It is true that without community of language there may be an artificial nationality, a nationality which may be good for political purposes, and which may engender a common national feeling. Still this is not quite the same thing as that fuller national unity which is felt where there is community of language. In fact, mankind instinctively takes language as the badge of nationality."

Pursuing the thought and reverting to the Greeks, I am tempted to take an example from Herodotus of what Athens could do in her nobler moods. Secretly dreading her power of resistance after Marathon and Salamis, but after all Attica had been overrun and devastated, Mardonius sought to detach her from the alliance of those communities which still remained faithful to the common cause. Fearful that the bribes and flatteries of the Persian might prevail, Sparta sent her ambassadors who met at the same moment with those of Mardonius, and their respective interests were openly debated in the presence of Athenians. After hearing both, the Athenians replied, first to the Persians, or their representative ally, Alexander of Macedon:

"We know as well as thou dost that the power of the Mede is many times greater than our own; we did not need to have that cast in our teeth. Nevertheless we cling so to freedom that we shall offer what resistance we may. Seek not to persuade us into making terms with the barbarians; say what thou wilt, thou wilt never gain our assent. Return rather at once and tell Mardonius that our answer to him is this: So long as the sun keeps his present course we will never join alliance with Xerxes: Nay, we shall oppose him unceasingly, trusting in the aid of those gods and heroes whom he has lightly esteemed, whose houses and whose images he has burnt with fire. And come not thou again to us with words like these, nor, thinking to do us a service, persuade us to unholy actions. Thou art the guest and friend of our nation; we would not that thou shouldst receive hurt at our hands."[31]

And then, turning to the Spartans, they went on as follows:

"That the Lacedemonians should fear lest we should make terms with the barbarian was very natural; yet, knowing as you do the mind of Athenians, you appear to entertain an unworthy dread, for there is neither so much gold anywhere in the world, nor a country so pre-eminent in beauty and fertility by receiving which we should be willing to side with the Mede and enslave Greece. For there are many and powerful considerations that forbid us to do so, even if we were inclined. First and chief, the images and dwellings of the gods, burnt and laid in ru-

[30] *Race and Language,* p. 106.
[31] *Herodotus,* book viii., chap. cxliii. (Rawlinson).

ins: this we must needs avenge to the utmost of our power rather than make terms with the man who has perpetrated such deeds. Secondly, the Grecian race being of the *same blood and the same language* and the temples of the gods and sacrifices in common, and our customs being similar—for the Athenians to become betrayers of these would not be well. Know, therefore, if you did not know it before, that so long as one Athenian is left alive, we will never make terms with Xerxes. Your forethought, however, which you manifest towards us, we admire, in that you offer to provide for us whose property is thus ruined, so as to be willing to support our families, and you have fulfilled the duties of benevolence; we, however, will continue in the state we are without being burdensome to you. Now, since matters stand as they do, send out an army with all possible expedition; for, as we conjecture, the barbarian will in no long time be here again to invade our territories as soon as he shall hear our message that we will do none of the things he required of us. Therefore, before he has reached Attica, it is fitting that we go out to meet him in Bœotia."[32]

The passage and its application need no comment. It thrills our blood to-day, as it must have done those who spoke, and those who listened, two thousand four hundred years ago. Would that Greece could have always remained true to her grander instincts and motives!

IV.—THE SAME LITERATURE

In all the articles which we may examine upon the subject of alliance, the existence of a common literature is ranked as one of its main moving causes. I have not found that any of the advocates of Anglo-Saxon co-operation have elaborated this thought. They have rested with a mere statement of the proposition. Strongly self-evident as this seems, I am not satisfied to pass it over without some elaboration. I want to be certain that we all understand and appreciate the nature and degree of the influence of literature upon this proposed union. Why is literature an important, *natural* factor, in the proposed alliance? As I take it, it is because we gather most of our knowledge and mental training from the same intellectual fountainhead. English literature tells us how the English-American people think; it shows what their process and basis of reasoning and feeling are, upon all subjects, small and great. If we are the same in our ideas, we behold its reflection in this vast mirror of thought and opinion; if we are divergent, we know the reason; and as one of the most ordinary functions of literature is to state, explain, examine, and discuss, eventually we are brought to a closer basis of common thought.

Besides all this, our literature marks course of national life—retrogressive or progressive. It holds up in the widest sense the "glass of fashion and the mould of form."

Certainly, if a proposition were made to establish an alliance between France and the United States of America, or between Germany or Russia and the United States, the literature of these countries could not be appealed to, to establish a common tie or natural bond of sympathy between them. The Americans, as a people,

---

[32] *Herodotus*, book viii., chap. cxliv. (Rawlinson).

know as little of French literature as the French, German, or Russians know of English literature. The literature of each of these countries is as a sealed book, except to those who have the leisure and inclination for special studies. Different causes and motives would therefore have to be sought for, to support a proposition of union. In the case of the Anglo-Saxon people, however, it is otherwise; they read the same books, magazines, and papers; they feed on the same intellectual food. Words perish as soon as they are spoken. Literature never dies, but is transmitted from generation to generation without end or limit. The literature of a country is the expression not only of its actual knowledge, but also of its genius and natural character; and this is diffused through all channels of publication, by means of books, magazines, and papers. Whenever this manifestation finds a lodgment in the minds of its readers, it is again transmitted by language. Literature, therefore, becomes a prolific source of instruction and education, and, as we drink from the same fountain of knowledge and inspiration, our tastes, habits, and modes of thought necessarily approximate to each other. An individual reads for pleasure or instruction, and what he receives of either or both combined, he again readily imparts by speech or pen to whomsoever he meets; hence literature acts directly upon some, and indirectly upon all. The Anglo-Saxon people, through the medium of literature, are continuously *en rapport* with each other. Everything published in the English language becomes common property to the whole English-speaking world; giving rise, according to its degree of merit, to the same impressions; calling into exercise the same faculties and sensibilities. The influence of literature may be considered in direct connection with language, of which it is the growth, and which in its turn it amplifies, strengthens, and embellishes. But let us consider the matter a little more closely.

In point of quantity, the publications in the English language are said to exceed those of all the other nations of the earth combined. In point of scholarship, art in writing, eloquence, spirit, research, and knowledge, English literature is certainly second to none. It may be natural partiality arising from the native use of the language and more intimate acquaintance with the originals, but it is a conviction deeply rooted in the mind of the English reader, even the most scholarly, that his own literature is, upon the whole, the greatest that the ages have yet produced.

In its composite form, it is a link in the chain, binding together the present and the past. I do not now refer to the past of our own race, when we were all participating in its formation, but to what is properly known as antiquity. With many of the words and phrases, and much of the syntax and prosody of the ancient tongues, we have also imbibed much of their spirit—of what is properly designated the "classic." I am not one of those who belittle the classic; far from wishing to see it eliminated, I would wish to see it cultivated. With all the native strength of the "English," there was ample room for the infusion of the graces and proprieties of the Greek and Latin.[33]

Out of the development of the languages so blended sprung variety, harmony, style, and, as a consequence, taste in composition. In every epoch of our literature,

[33] Read in this connection the address of Lord Brougham, when elected Lord Rector of the University of Glasgow, delivered April 9. 1825.

in each of its manifestations, from Gower and Chaucer to Tennyson and Longfellow, we find the presence of this classic attribute, first dim and struggling, then actual and triumphant, forming, moulding, beautifying, and perfecting. The benefits which our civilisation has derived from this process are incalculable. It would be a sorry day for us on both sides of the Atlantic when the common standards depending on taste in writing should be lost. Those of speech would soon follow, and the language would become a confused mass of barbarisms. The effects upon its character would soon be traced. I believe, from certain indications, that it will rest with us in the frequent fluctuations of changing style, to vindicate our title of depositories of the permanent models of the literature and language, by becoming also its preservers—in other words, to oppose a barrier to evident tendencies towards overgrowth, obscurity, and corruption. If so it be, the influence will be felt as a reflex one, extending backward to the shores where the language originated, and so again illustrating the invisible and indivisible tie that binds us together, "Old Ocean" to the contrary notwithstanding.

Our original Saxon tongue was not conquered by the Greek and Roman, as were those of the nations of the South of Europe; *it appropriated them*—leading them, as it were, in a kind of magnificent triumph. Out of the interfusion, such as it was, came a dialect and afterwards a literature, wholly *sui generis*. We find the same characteristic in the assimilation of the Roman civil law by our own common law. Our legal system did not become Latinised—but whatever was good, sound, and relevant in the civil law became incorporated and was Anglicised. In dwelling upon our literature for a moment, I shall not, as is usually done, glorify particular names—Spenser, Shakespeare, the dramatists, Milton, Bacon, Hooker, Jeremy Taylor, Burke, the classicists so-called. All the long array of great thinkers, eloquent preachers, exquisite poets, and novelists will occur at once to everyone. Let me rather dwell, as more germane to our present purpose, upon certain traits common to all, notwithstanding the diversities of styles and epochs. I would mention, then, as one such trait, a certain solidity of thought—a something derived from the actual experience of life and close experimental contact with nature. This is visible at all times, and impresses one as quite in keeping with that other something in the character of the people (if the two can be at all separated), which has led to the creation and preservation of their political institutions. It is certainly a native quality, being equally characteristic of the very loftiest and most fervent productions of English genius, and of those which have no other claim upon us than sober good sense. Carrying the thought a little farther, these observations of man and nature become a positive force in the formation of individual character, and, of course, of society. It is this sure, well-grounded, *homelike* quality which, among all the other literatures of the world, peculiarly distinguishes the English, united as it may be and has been in many instances, with the utmost perfection of art. It is to detract from an almost universal characteristic to cite instances, but what other literature has productions like the *Pilgrim's Progress, Robinson Crusoe*, or poetry in this respect like Cowper's *Task?* What is Shakespeare but a revelation of familiar thought and feeling sublimed by genius? What is Milton, classicist as he is, in the garden scenes of Paradise, but the painter of an English home? The very flowers of *his* Paradise seem made to bloom there. Addison and all the essayists,—in what does their charm consist, but in their communion with daily life and thought? So, too, as to their legitimate successors, the great novelists. The new world they have given us—what is it but an accurate representation of the men and women we have known, and a delightful participation in all their experiences? Truly we have a rich and ever-abiding inheritance in this literature. The inheritance itself is a positive gift, but it is more. It points out infallibly the direction our minds should take in dealing with those from whom we have derived it. With such a genuine emanation before us of the mental, moral, political, and religious life of a people, shall we go amiss in extending to them our sympathies and establishing a mutual friendship? In this way we know them—know them as we can in no other way—not through the obscuring haze of momentary passion, and the disturbance of abnormal aberrations, but through a medium deep as the life of nations and of universal binding efficacy. If language and literature have made us one, by what unhallowed process shall we be "put asunder"?

I have used the word "English" in reference to literature following the common style; of course I include our own. In all that is best, it shows the common origin. Franklin, the Federalist; the great indigenous Webster, who knew so well "what blood flowed in his veins";[34]

"I am happy to stand here to-day and to remember that, although my ancestors, for several generations, lie buried beneath the soil of the Western Continent, yet there has been a time when my ancestors and your ancestors toiled in the same cities and villages, cultivated adjacent fields, and worked together to build up that great structure of civil polity which has made England what England is."

The refined and genial Irving—and all our later names are classed together in thought;—a noble republic free from enmity and faction, in which they march under one banner and shed a single influence. An English boy recites *The Song of Marion's Men*, with as much enthusiasm as an American. Longfellow is a household name in England as with us; Emerson was received in Oxford and Cambridge as a "new light" along with Newman and Carlyle. The time is not far distant, if we will be true to ourselves, when America will be classic ground to the Englishman, as, long since, Irving declared, England was to America. *I have not been able to perceive that there lingers in the English mind one trace of the old-time disparagement of American books, things, and manners.* Candid and just criticism they may employ towards us, as to themselves; that right is inalienable and it has its uses; but their praise is more frequent than their censure, and being accompanied by discernment, has more value. English criticism has sometimes made a classic reputation for our authors— as in the case of Poe and Hawthorne. Walt Whitman is more curiously and tolerantly read there than among ourselves. As we have developed, the disposition has grown to accord us a full appreciation. At no time whatever, though half-serious, half-humorous badinage may have existed, has there ever been a particle of envy.

I thus place before the English-American people some of the influences of a common literature. Pursue the subject as we may, through all its ramifications, the stronger becomes the conviction of its power to unite us for good and noble

---

[34] Speech at Oxford, *Works*, vol. i., p. 438.

purposes.[35]

V.—THE SAME POLITICAL INSTITUTIONS

In the formation of the Constitution of the United States the theory and spirit, substance and form, of the political institutions of England were most strikingly followed. Here is another natural bond of sympathy, fellowship, and nationality, of the strongest nature between these countries.

A brief review of the cardinal points in the political development of the English-speaking people seems an essential feature of this aspect of the question.

More than eight centuries elapsed between the reign of Alfred the Great, and the "Bill of Rights," in the reign of William and Mary (875 to 1688), In all this time, the English people were steadily and constantly engaged in building and perfecting their present system of government.

It was a fabric of slow and often unconscious growth, and many times when it seemed to be on the verge of completion, the storms of rebellion, of kingly usurpations, of foreign wars, swept fiercely through its walls and blew them to the ground. These very storms were instruments in regular and organic development; and, nothing discouraged or disheartened, the people bravely set to work, and commenced again the task of rebuilding and finishing the great governmental edifice, which they were to leave to the world as an imperishable monument of their courage, hardihood, love of freedom and justice, and which should, in all time, prove a refuge and an asylum for the oppressed and liberty-loving people of the world.

The foundations of this government were not completed in the reign of Alfred—when the different kingdoms which prevailed in England were fast approaching consolidation.

The germs of an executive power are faintly foreshadowed in the personal influence of the reigning King, whose authority vacillated as the King himself was strong or weak. But the war with the Northmen raised Alfred and his sons from tribal leaders to national kings, and the dying out of other royal stocks left the house of Cerdic the one line of hereditary kingship.[36]

The seeds of parliamentary birth were steadily growing in the form of a Witenagemote, in the "great meeting" of the Assembly of the wise—which represented the whole English people, as the wise moots of each kingdom represented the separate peoples of each, its powers being as supreme in the wider field as theirs in the narrower, all developing from the people as they were arranged in

[35] "England," says Mr. Carlyle, "before long, this Island of ours, will hold but a small fraction of the English; in America, in New Holland, east and west to the very Antipodes, there will be a *Saxondom* covering great spaces of the globe. And now, what is it that can keep all these together into virtually one Nation, so that they do not fall-out and fight, but live at peace, in brother-like intercourse, helping one-another? . . . Yes, this Shakspeare is ours; we produce him, we speak and think by him; we are of one blood and one kind with him. The most common-sense politician, too, if he pleases, may think of that."

[36] Green's *History of the English People*, vol. i., p. 91.

their local Assemblies or Hundreds.[37] For to it belonged the higher justice, the power to impose taxes, the making of laws, the conclusion of treaties, the control of wars, the disposal of public lands, the appointment of great officers of state, and, finally, it could elect or depose a king.[38]

It is not within the limits or sphere of my purpose to go into the details, but when Alfred died the fundamental principles of a sound and substantial government existed, illustrated in an executive, legislative, and judicial department clearly defined.

Besides this feature of his reign, a commercial activity began to be developed, and literary tastes and education encouraged and cultivated.

The free institutions of Alfred survived under the Norman tyranny or conquest. No substantial change was made in law or custom by William.[39]

The germs of the famous Magna Charta were laid in the reign of Henry I., and almost one of the first acts of this monarch was to grant a charter which was calculated to remedy many of the grievous oppressions which had been committed during the reigns of his father, William the Conqueror, and his brother, William Rufus.

The example of Henry, in granting a charter favourable to the liberties of the people, was followed by Stephen, who renewed the grant, which was confirmed by Henry II. But the concessions of these princes were one thing and their actions another. They still continued to exercise the same unlimited authority.

The charter of John, Magna Charta, culminated the people's expressions of their wrongs. That its provisions were not novel or startling, that the people knew exactly what they wanted, is strongly manifest from the asserted fact that this great and famous *constitution* was finally discussed and agreed to in a *single* day.[40]

I say "constitution," for the Magna Charta was in form and substance as much a constitution as that which the thirteen States of North America adopted in 1789. It defined and limited the power of the Executive; it provided for the constitution and assembling of a legislative body in a general council—a Parliament; it regulated the general principles of judicial power; and, finally, it was, from beginning *to* end, a bill of rights for the people of England high and low—of all classes. It is interesting in this connection to draw a parallel:

First: The Charter names the *parties* between whom it was made. John, the party on the *one side*, and his Archbishops, Bishops, Abbots, Earls, Barons, Justiciaries, Foresters, Sheriffs, Governors, Officers, all Bailiffs, and his *faithful subjects*, the parties on *the other side.*

The Constitution of the United States with more brevity, but with equal comprehensiveness, proclaims that its provisions are for the *people* of the United States.

[37] Green's *History of the English People*, vol. i., p. 91.

[38] *Ibid.*

[39] Reeves's *History of the English Law*, by Finlason, p. 230. Green's *English People*, vol. i., p. 116.

[40] Green's *English People*, vol. i., p. 244,

Second: Magna Charta was a grant from a King—or, more correctly, an acknowledgment ok deed of confirmation from a King—clearly enumerating the rights of the people, and the nature of the compact between them. It was accordingly sealed by John, and attested by a cloud of attending witnesses. It was coerced from him by an aroused people—at their risk, with arms in their hands.

The Constitution of the United States was an agreement between thirteen independent States, establishing a federative nation, and duly signed by the representative of each State on behalf of the people.

Third: The Charter of John deals with the rights to things and the rights of persons. Many of these rights, being regulated by the laws of the States of the Union, do not appear in the Constitution of the United States, but are reserved by the States.

Fourth: Article First of the Constitution of the United States creates, apportions, and regulates the legislative power of the Government with clearness and precision. A paragraph of Magna Charta provides for the holding of the general Council consisting of Archbishops, Bishops, Abbots, Earls, and greater Barons of the realm to be summoned "singly by our letters." This, however, as well as Alfred's Witenagemote, answered rather the idea of a great council—it was an aristocratic body—the origin of the House of Lords: all that was possible at that day.

It further provides for the summoning generally, by "our sheriffs and bailiffs, all others who hold of us in chief (tenants *in capite*) forty days" before their meeting at least, and to a certain place, the cause of the summons being declared, and the business to proceed on the day appointed.

Henry III., in 1258-59, called together the Barons in Parliament, who in turn ordered that four Knights should be chosen of each county; that they should make inquiry into grievances of which their neighbourhood had reason to complain, and should attend the ensuing Parliament, in order to give information to that Assembly of the state of their particular counties. This is a nearer approach to the present Parliament than had been made by the Barons in the reign of King John, and was the beginning of the House of Commons.[41]

By paragraph XII. of the Great Charter it was further provided that no scutage or aid (in other words, taxation) should be imposed, unless by the General Council of the Kingdom. This principle was strongly reiterated in the Petition of Right (1628).

Fifth: Magna Charta was a limitation of kingly power by the aristocracy, but distinctively in favour of the people. The "Barons' War" in Henry Third's reign, resulted in the full establishment of the representative system of government, *i.e.,* the House of Commons.

The separation from the Church of Rome, as an instrument of government, quite independent of any religious point of view, secured laws, liberty, government, and freedom from foreign domination.

The approach to a popular system under the House of Lancaster, and the reac-

[41] Hume's *History of England*, vol. i., pp. 549-550.

tion towards despotism under the Tudors, growing out of their peculiar historical situation, was again followed by a powerful reaction towards liberty under the Stuarts. The expulsion of the latter was followed by the establishment of a constitutional system under William III., embracing, among other things,

a. The declaration of rights.

b. Religious toleration (in the main).

c. The distinct recognition of the *habeas corpus* act enacted under Charles II.

d. The germ of a ministry responsible directly to parliament and indirectly to the people.

e. Freedom of speech and the press.

From all which great and *wholly* self-derived institutions were created the instrumentalities of all political progress, both at home and abroad. Holland, it is true, had tolerations, but they were no less of native English growth.

Thus step by step can be traced the building of this great political edifice, whose architecture was so closely followed by our own American Constitution-builders.

The fundamental distinction between the English Government, as portrayed and developed in Magna Charta, the Petition of Right, and Bill of Rights, and the Constitution of the United States, is that the aim of the former instruments was to define and limit the powers of the monarch; while the latter sought at once to create, specify, and restrict the authority of the Federal Government. Both attempted to define and preserve the rights of the people. The main objects are one; the divergencies are the natural result of the prevailing conditions of both countries. The distinctive aim of English political development has been to obtain its objects by enlarging the powers of Parliament, while the fundamental purpose of the American people was to make a general government so constituted as to preserve both the rights of the States and people. These correlative purposes are remarkably illustrated in the method of construction, for by Magna Charta it is provided, "It is also sworn as well on our part as on the part of the Barons that all of the things aforesaid shall be observed in good faith and without evil subtility"—and in the Constitution of the United States it is set forth in effect that the Imperium is to be created, and then that the "powers not delegated to the United States by the Constitution—nor prohibited by it to the States, are reserved to the States respectively, or to the people "; the States being the reservoirs of all the free principles conferred by them out of their abundance on the general government.

Substantially all the powers which were conceded to belong to the monarch by these organic instruments, and by the political records of England, were specifically conferred by the Constitution of the United States upon the President.

Before the commencement of the War of 1776, the first volume of Blackstone's *Commentaries* was published and in the hands of all the American lawyers. The chapters upon the powers of Parliament and the prerogative of, and restrictions upon, kingly authority, were fully and perspicuously set forth therein. Here was the fountain from which much of the inspiration of the American Constitution makers was drawn. The influence of Blackstone and its predecessor, the *Spirit of*

Law, by Montesquieu, both before and after the Revolution, was very great. Nor do I overlook the influence which arose from a study of Grecian history by some of its framers—although their studies were said to be somewhat superficial.[42]

Our Bill of Rights, which was not adopted until after the Constitution had been inaugurated, but which appears as the first ten amendments to that instrument, was almost literally copied from the Petition of Right, presented in the reign of Charles I., by Parliament (1628) and the Bill of Rights of 1689.

The Constitution of the United States contains new matter, especially as regards the delicate relation of the States to each other and to the newly constituted government, not to be found in Magna Charta, or in the Petition, or Bill of' Rights, growing as it did out of the necessity of providing for a new condition of affairs, but in everything fundamental and substantial relating to the legislative, judicial, and executive branches of the government, it has faithfully followed the principles of the English Constitution.

With the American appropriation and assimilation of these inherited political ideas, there exists language, literature, and all the rest of the kindred sympathies, making a tie stronger than blood, and culminating in the grand conception of federation developed into government, *i.e.,* the Constitution of the United States.

Mr. Gladstone unites the view of the English and American Constitutions in the oft-quoted words "as the British Constitution is the most subtle organism which has proceeded from progressive history, so the American Constitution is the most wonderful work ever struck off at a given time by the brain and purpose of man."

Who should acknowledge the value of all this, and the sacrifices which it has cost England, if not we, who have inherited it, fed upon it, grown upon it, and to-day livingly embody and exemplify it?

Is not sympathy and brotherhood between the two peoples, the natural, necessary, and inevitable outcome? "Whom God hath joined together let no man put asunder."

VI.—THE SAME LAWS, LEGAL CUSTOMS, AND GENERAL MODES OF JUDICIAL PROCEDURE

Closely allied to, if not a part of their political institutions, comes another natural feature of the alliance, an element more powerful than steel to rivet the bonds between the two nations, *i.e.,* the same laws, customs, and general modes of legal procedure.

The phenomenal and colossal development of North America is somewhat explained by the fact that we were not compelled to create or originate our political institutions, laws, or judicial modes of procedure; these were all ready for us when we commenced the business of an independent government. The materials were at hand with which we were to build the grand structure of democracy. Whatever difficulty was experienced in the design, whatever time was spent in the building,

[42] Freeman's *History of Federal Government in Greece and Italy,* 2nd Edition, p. 249.

was attributable to the jealousies, fears and anxieties of the delegates who represented the thirteen original independent States in the Constitutional Convention. The great and almost insurmountable barrier to the creation of the Republic arose out of an inability to agree to a common basis of association on becoming members of the same family, and surrendering the independent and supreme rights of sovereignty which each of the contracting parties possessed. As colonies we knew no law but the common law; we profited by its utility; we imbibed its teachings; no study was more general among the people. After the Union had become a *fait accompli*, in most of the States it was solemnly adjudged to remain in force. A new field, corresponding to the growth and importance of the country, was opened to its influence, both here and in England. The two countries now mutually profit by each other in this respect, finding a never-failing source of legal illumination, not only in their judicial precedents and statutory enactments, but in the many admirable text-books—critical, expository and historical, which deal with almost every conceivable subject of private or public rights and duties, in all their practical and ethical relations. Thus that mighty instrumentality, the Law, remains substantially the same in both countries.

We fought the battles of the Revolution to become an independent nation, but when we were free we established New England; we voluntarily adopted every important principle of public and private jurisprudence of the Mother country, and clothed ourselves anew with her legal and judicial garments. The materials of which our governmental house was built, the legal furniture which was used in its embellishment and decoration, we took from the well-stored warehouse of English institutions, and Gladstone's eulogy, which I have quoted above, is no less deserved because the builders of this new government assimilated the architecture and appropriated the materials of existing political institutions and legal principles to their new structure.

But we would be a strange people—wholly careless of history, utterly indifferent to our own political genealogy, if we did not realise and appreciate this splendid record which England had been making through bloody sacrifices and internal struggles for more than twelve centuries—from the reign of Alfred the Great to that of William III., the fruits of which were so fully utilised and enjoyed by us in the establishment of our government. I am not stopping to coin eulogies. I am simply pointing out the facts—facts of supreme importance, but which from their very obviousness have been too easily lost sight of.

But it is just to remark in this connection, that the framers of our Constitution did not blindly, heedlessly, and mechanically copy the English models. Every principle was submitted to the test of severe and analytical argument, every plank that entered into the construction of the Ship of State was thoroughly examined and shown to be sound before it was put into its appropriate place. As the artists and architects model from the works of Angelo and Raphael so the men who fashioned our organic law intelligently studied, assimilated, and applied the principles of the English Constitution to our own government. They showed an artistic, profound, and delicate exercise of judgment, an almost divine perception of the purposes and necessities of the people in the selection of the materials for the laws of the country. These necessities were found to be fully provided for in the legal archives of the old government, which we were simply expanding.

In a few instances we did not adopt their laws.

For example, in the rule applicable to the descent of real property, the Americans struck out the doctrine of primogeniture, but substantially adopted the entire body of English law appertaining to real estate. The law forms; the procedure; the principles applicable to the rights of persons and things; criminal law, equity jurisprudence, were taken *en bloc*, with exceptions too trifling to be mentioned.

The rules, principles, and forms of English jurisprudence were so fitted to the spirit and genius of our people, that (with but several trifling exceptions, such as a few small treatises on Justices' Courts and Sheriffs), after the adoption of our Constitution, there was not a single elementary treatise of American Law published in the United States until 1826 — at which time Kent's *Commentaries* made its appearance, and it is remarkable that, as legal science has advanced in this country, the prejudices of its professors have softened towards the country from which its materials have been chiefly drawn.

VII.—THE SAME TENDENCY AND METHODS OF RELIGIOUS THOUGHT AND WORSHIP

In both the British Empire and the United States, there is an official, and an almost universal, recognition of a superhuman power to whom allegiance and service are regarded as justly due. This is religion in a broad, comprehensive sense.

In each nation we find instances of cruel and unjustifiable religious intolerance and persecution; but the tendency has always been towards liberality and religious freedom.

In no other nation upon the globe does religion flourish in all its forms and sects as in these countries.

Without agreement or imitation, we find the march of religious freedom keeping about the same pace in each nation.

What does this prove? The same religious impulses, thoughts, freedom, education, and growth; a family physically disunited, with one religious conception moulding their convictions in the same groove of thought. In England and the United States, for example, the Catholic religion flourishes and expands even more than in those countries where it is the established and official worship! Every branch of Protestantism is encouraged and grows in this congenial soil of English liberty. Religious independence and toleration are conspicuously planted in the heart of every true Anglo-Saxon. We can point with pride, on the one hand, to the toleration of rationalistic views upon religious subjects; and, on the other, to the growth and expansion of Christianity, and their joint influence upon our progress and civilisation.

Anglo-Saxon unity, strength, and progress owe, perhaps, as much to Christianity in all its forms, as to any other cause. It ought to be one of the most potent influences towards the unification of the Anglo-Saxon people. No nobler topic can occupy the attention of the pulpit.

VIII.—INTERMARRIAGES

Following the growth of other influences is intermarriage. Every day it becomes more frequent. It is not difficult for the individuals of the one country to become members of the homes of the other, and, as the Atlantic now only affords the opportunity of a pleasant excursion, whatever there was of physical isolation in the past has almost disappeared. Female influence is here seen performing its salutary work to the best advantage in removing prejudice and harmonising opinions and manners. Such all-important instrumentalities act with a sort of geometrical aggregation, and constitute one of the surest means of making us all members of one great household.

IX.—OTHER SIMILARITIES BETWEEN THE TWO NATIONS, EXHIBITING THE NATURAL FEATURES OF THE ALLIANCE, SUCH AS THE DRAMA, SPORTS, PASTIMES, HABITS OF LIVING

From all these sources there flow influences which increase the volume and strength of the movement towards unification.

Let us advert briefly to the drama. Besides its influence as literature, it forms, in its visual representation, no unimportant part in shaping the affinities of the two countries. What more potent influence can be conceived in this respect than the mighty Shakespeare? And so through the long list of his contemporaries and successors. Whatever has been seen on the stage becomes at once the common property of both peoples. The interchange so afforded of the varying types of the same manners and ideas—the very personalities of the performers—has been an agency no less certain than subtle in moulding the two peoples into one. And it may be noticed, in proof of this, how instantly we detect the stamp of foreign thought and manners, when any play that is *not English* is represented.

Why should I dwell upon this phase of the subject? Simply to show that, do what we may, we cannot unfamiliarise ourselves—we cannot escape from our natural tendencies. Suppose it were suggested that the United States should establish a common and perpetual relation with some foreign nation other than England? Could we invoke any of these natural elements of sympathy and bonds of relationship to support the movement? Suppose it were proposed to consolidate France and England? Or France and the United States? Or Russia and England? Or the United States and Russia? Is it not evident, at least at this stage of their development, that the union or coalition would be unnatural? In sports, pastimes, drama, habits of living, how utterly irreconcilable are the Russians and English? In all phases of their individual and national life, in their moral, political, and religious education and sentiments, there are constantly cropping out all kinds of diversities and incongruities. Oil and water will not commingle.

X.—RÉSUMÉ

Finally, to sum up and put these thoughts together; to aggregate the *natural* elements which would render a national marriage between the United States and England justifiable, healthful, and prosperous, we find that we are of the same family; we speak the same language; we have the same literature; we are governed substantially by the same political institutions; we possess similar laws, customs, and general modes of legal procedure; we follow the same tendency and methods of religious thought and practice; we have numerous inter-marriages and innumerable similarities in our sports, pastimes, drama, and habits of living—a natural community in everything important.

Pursue the English and Americans into their homes, into their churches, into their courts, and political institutions; into their business and commercial lives; into their theatres, amusements, and pastimes, we shall discover that we all "live, move, and have our being" according to the same general principles and methods of thought.

Are not the foundations of an international relation, when made of such materials, solid and secure? Is not a tree planted in such congenial soil sure to grow and bear noble fruit?

CHAPTER V

THE SELFISH CAUSES WHICH PROVOKE AND SUPPORT AN ALLIANCE, EXAMINED

I NOW pass into another sphere of thought not less important than the one I have just left, but where the motives found are of a purely selfish and practical nature. It is said that the foundation of all human action is either sympathy or selfishness.[43] I have appealed to the first, I now invoke the common interests of the two nations—a selfish motive, but one of inestimable importance in the study of the question of an Anglo-Saxon union.

I.—THE COMMON INTERESTS OF BOTH COUNTRIES DEMAND CO-OPERATION—IDENTITY OF INTERNATIONAL ACTION

It is with nations as with individuals; the larger and more valuable the commercial relations grow, the greater necessity there is for close, frank, and cordial ties between them. The heart must follow the pocket. While the laws of business are based upon inexorable principles of supply and demand, and the efforts of producers must be to sell to consumers the best goods at the lowest prices, which stimulates rivalry and trade, yet two men cannot be successful partners in commercial affairs unless they act in perfect sympathy and accord. Nor can a merchant retain his customers unless there be a certain amount of mutual confidence and respect existing between them. Close international relations with our best customer, therefore, appeal directly to our interest—to our pockets.

I wish in this connection to recall a piece of history, unknown to some, overlooked by others, and ignored by most of us. I do not use it as a makeweight—but only as exhibiting one phase of our development. It was with the aid of English capital that our commercial life in its broad sense began. English financial support originally enabled us to open and build up our country; to attain a point where our phenomenal and natural conditions propelled our advance without outside aid. Whether English capital sought investment and expected profit to result therefrom—an expectation many, many times unfulfilled, it was her money which we used to aid in our development by the opening of this great country through large and small systems of railroad and water communications.

Even if we had paid all these advances, which we have not, we should not

---

[43] See *Buckle*, vol. ii., p. 334 *et seq.*

forget it was English and not French or Russian money which sent us moving towards great national prosperity; and while this consideration is not paramount it should count for something in this discussion.

Commercial relations

Financial relations

Once begun, the commercial and financial relations of the two countries have broadened and deepened until, to-day, they are so intricate and immense that we are practically one mercantile community. We are partners and co-helpers in finance, industry, and commerce. It is not necessary to cite full statistics. They are known, and have been used to cover every phase of our commercial history. We are commercially and financially so intertwined that it is impossible to unravel the cords of interest that bind us together.

Exports of merchandise from the United States for the year ending June 30,

	1899	1900	1901
Into the United Kingdom	$511,778,705	$533,829,374	$631,266,263
Into all other parts of Europe.	424,823,388	506,337,938	504,825,997

Imports of merchandise into the United States for the year ending June 30,

	1899	1900	1901
From the United Kingdom	$118,488,217	$159,583,060	$143,365,901
From all other parts of Europe.	235,396,317	280,926,420	286,070,279[44]

Pure interest, therefore, is always at work to cement and tighten our relations with England; and in testing the motives which influence human conduct, which one can be found stronger than self-interest?

II.—SELF-PRESERVATION—PROTECTION—NECESSITY

Of the different motives which individuals or nations invoke to defend or justify their actions, none are higher, or more universally recognised than those of self-preservation—protection—necessity—which are interchangeable terms.

Self-preservation is a broad and essential attribute of individual and national existence. It is not confined to a mere present danger, but extends to the future, and anticipates evils which are growing or maturing; it scents the approach of danger and prepares for it in advance.

The people of the United States are unconscious of any present external danger, and perhaps none exists. But it is a very short-sighted and foolish policy to confine our politics and diplomacy to mere present conditions. The brightest sunshine is followed by the gloomiest skies. The Spanish War revealed what a European alliance against us without England's aid might mean. The very wisdom of to-day, therefore, forces us to look into futurity. It is simple prudence to cast our

[44]   Review of the World's Commerce, issued from the Bureau of Foreign Commerce, Department of State, Washington, D. C., 1902.

eyes around the civilised world, and study and endeavour to comprehend the movements and directions of the other political bodies. Are not our motions as a nation jealously and eagerly watched by the European powers? While we are secure now, is it safe to assume that we shall always be? England, on the other hand, is in daily peril. She is the target for all European combinations. Envy and hatred pursue her hourly,—very causeless envy and hatred, as it seems to me, or, if not causeless, arising only from that spirit of legitimate enterprise in which we again are so much like her. To whom should she look in a moment of real danger? In what direction should she cast her eyes? Should it not be upon her own family,—her own offspring? Are we so blind that we cannot see that the decimation or destruction of England's power is a blow to ourselves? And what position would we occupy with the combined powers against us, with England as their ally, or acting as a neutral, or (what is most horrible to conceive) powerless to aid us?

What is the present preponderating duty of our people? Is it not to encourage, extend, and protect the Anglo-Saxon race wherever it is to be found?

The principle of self-preservation is plain and universally recognised; the occasion and necessity for its application are equally clear. The salvation and perpetuation of the Anglo-Saxon race furnishes a powerful, if not a preponderating motive for perfect accord between the United States and the British Empire.

The expansion and preservation of the race are to be attained only by union, which self-interest inspires. The failure to adopt it is an act of *felo de se.*

III.—DUTY

I have said before, in substance,[45] that a nation has a duty to perform to itself and to the outside world, precisely as an individual has a duty to fulfil to himself and his fellow-beings. The entire limit of either's obligation is not performed by simply attending to his own selfish needs.

The more civilised we are the clearer this duty is enjoined. As Demosthenes said: "To a Democracy nothing is more essential than scrupulous regard to equity and justice." A nation does not exist merely for pure selfishness—or simply to protect the lives, enhance the fortunes, and secure the happiness of its own immediate citizens. It cannot erect a wall around its people and live entirely within itself. This is as unnatural as it is impossible. There must be intercommunion with other powers and peoples. To render its full duty to its citizens, there must be intermingling with outside nations. Through these means its own people become richer, more prosperous, and cultivated, and the nations with whom it associates benefit proportionately from the intercourse. *With us there can be no such thing as national isolation.* Especially is this remark applicable to the United States *at this time;* on the eve of embarking upon a colonial policy. Our hands once placed upon a colony can never be withdrawn. This is one of the characteristics of the Anglo-Saxon race and in our case strongly supported by duty. We shall benefit the colonists in all ways, but they will remain part of our system until it is dissolved.

Our duty, growing out of the best and noblest conceptions of the origin and

[45] *Ante,* p. 62 *et seq.*

purpose of social existence, should teach us, along with our material interests and often by means of them, to propagate and extend everywhere the principles upon which our civilisation is founded.

I do not mean that this thought should inspire conquest—for mere enlargement of territory or other aggrandisement. On the contrary, in our dealings with and treatment of other nations, the abstract principles of right should never be forgotten.

But, wherever we land in our national pilgrimage, either by conquest or purchase, we must reign supreme.

I take it for granted that our views upon these subjects are the most humane and liberal. At least this is our great boast. We claim to lead civilisation. Is this assumption justified? The history of our lives from our national birth until the present time must be appealed to.[46] It is perhaps true that we have not always lived up to our ideals, but these ideals have never been destroyed. They may have been obscured, but the clouds which covered them have lifted again, and they have reappeared in their original vigour and beauty. It seems to be a marked characteristic of an Anglo-Saxon to propagate and push his principles everywhere. Without boasting, unconsciously, he goes on to the mark, and often with an appearance of cynical indifference. Inwardly he is not content unless all whom he meets participate in his enlightenment, and when it becomes in any degree difficult or impracticable, it may be assumed that the fault is not wholly his. Where racial or other antagonism is so pronounced as to render assimilation impossible, there is at least the minimum of evil in the onward march to a higher plane. The idea of most other nations is to limit their national principles to themselves. They seem to take no real interest in sowing their political seeds in foreign soils. Their objects are purely selfish.

It is our contention that the influence of the Anglo-Saxon race has been for good everywhere; that its principles have found lodgment in some form or other in all governments; that its laws and customs have percolated more or less into all political systems; and that all existing political bodies have in substance, if not in form, consciously or unconsciously engrafted into their systems some of the notions and principles of liberty and justice as applied by the English-speaking people. England has been called, and truly, "the mother of constitutions and the constitutional system." Our principles of national and individual liberty are so inseparable from true government that where they are not found, a real, beneficial, political institution does not exist.

As Mr. Webster said[47]:

"Now, Gentlemen, I do not know what practical views or what practical results may take place from this great expansion of the power of the two branches of Old England. It is not for me to say; I only can see, that on this continent all is to

---

[46] *Ante*, p. 71 *et seq.*

[47] Speech of Daniel Webster, delivered on the 22nd of December, 1843, at the Public Dinner of the New England Society of New York, in Commemoration of the Landing of the Pilgrims.

be Anglo-American from Plymouth Rock to the Pacific seas, from the north pole to California. That is certain; and in the Eastern world I only see that you can hardly place a finger on a map of the world and be an inch from an English settlement. Gentlemen, if there be anything in the supremacy of races, the experiment now in progress will develop it. If there be any truth in the idea that those who issued from the great Caucasian fountain, and spread over Europe, are to react on India and on Asia, and to act on the whole Western world, it may not be for us, nor our children, nor our grandchildren to see it, but it will be for our descendants of some generation to see the extent of that progress and dominion of the favoured races. For myself, I believe there is no limit fit to be assigned to it by the human mind, because I find at work everywhere, on both sides of the Atlantic, under various forms and degrees of restriction on the one hand, and under various degrees of motive and stimulus on the other hand, and in these branches of a common race, the great principle of *the freedom of human thought and the respectability of individual character* . . . I find everywhere an elevation of the character of man as man, an elevation of the individual as a component part of society; I find everywhere a rebuke of the idea that the many are made for the few, or that government is anything but an *agency* for mankind. And I care not beneath what zone, frozen, temperate, or torrid; I care not what complexion, white or brown; I care not under what circumstances of climate or cultivation, if I can find a race of men on an inhabitable spot of earth whose general sentiment it is, and whose general feeling it is, that government is made for man—man as a religious, moral, and social being—and not man for government, there I know that I shall find prosperity and happiness."

Following in the wake of these premises, therefore, arises our duty to propagate Anglo-Saxon principles; to increase and multiply its peoples; to strengthen and extend its influences; to carry its banners everywhere a human foot can tread and human energy be felt.

Some may think that their interests concur with their prejudices to prevent the union of the Anglo-Saxon people, no matter in what form, or for what object, the alliance is created. It would be difficult to define these interests, but whether they be real or unreal, substantial or immaterial, no attention should be given to any opposition supposedly arising out of them. If we are actuated by pure motives, which are made clear and are understood, we shall emerge from the struggle as the race always has, in victory.

And thus we have linked to the *natural; sympathetic* influences which operate to bring us closer together, the elements of *self-interest* and *self-preservation, protection*, and *necessity*; and, finally, to crown all, a high and mighty *duty*.

Here are centred all the motives of selfishness and all the influences of sympathy which are necessary to create and permanently continue a great political intermarriage,—a combination and a form indeed upon which "every god did seem to set his seal" to give the world the assurance of a great, prosperous and imperishable union.

CHAPTER VI

THE MEANS BY WHICH A CLOSER UNION MAY BE CREATED AND MAINTAINED

PRELIMINARY

I HAVE already spoken of the ineffectiveness, in truth I should say the hollowness, of mere expressions of good feeling, of the airy and fleeting *entente cordiale*, between the English and American people, arising out of temporary enthusiasm — or sentimental passion.[48]

On the other hand, I have discarded as wholly impracticable and dangerous a fixed, definite, written treaty of alliance—defensive and offensive. The people break away from the former, and the latter exists only until some temporary or imaginary selfish purpose or interest requires it to be broken. Is there not some medium, conservative ground between a sentimental *entente* and a written alliance which will indissolubly unite the Anglo-Saxon race in national sympathy and purpose? Let us consider this aspect of the subject.

I admit that some preparation must be made in the minds of the people of our race; that seeds must be sown in the ground of public opinion before a conclusion can be reached between the Anglo-Saxons upon this important subject. But these are times for quick action, — events mature soon, — and the last few years have been prolific in conditions which have opened the eyes and ripened the judgment of the English-speaking people. We have been brought close together by the instrumentalities of steam, electricity, and science; our commercial interests have interlocked us in a thousand ways; we have had the experience of the Spanish War; frequent intermingling has made us better acquainted with each other; in one word, the experiences of the last five years have done more to unite us as a people than all our combined antecedent history. The scales have dropped from

[48] Take the history of the Anglo-American League (*ante* p. 57) as an illustration of such sporadic influences and their results. That League was formed in London during the Spanish-American War. It was hailed in the United States with expressions of keen delight. But, the war ended, American enthusiasm oozed out; the Boer War began, manifestations were had in the United States against England, the whole efforts of the League were neutralised, if not frustrated, and the wishers for a real union between the countries sadly demoralised. The League is now almost forgotten, and many of its most respectable members are quite willing to conceal the fact that such a society ever existed. Yet the motives of its formation were noble and unselfish; its membership highly respectable and influential; but it confined its acts to mere *resolutions*; it was inspired by fleeting sentimental conditions.

our eyes as if by a miracle, and we can now regard ourselves in the mirror of our true interest and destiny.

I accordingly claim that the time and the people are alike ripe for some *action* which will tend to establish an indissoluble relation. It would be an ideal condition if we could act together for ever without the stroke of a pen—inspired by mere affection and sympathy; but the chain moulded in the fires of sentiment, no matter how effective in some regards, is not strong enough to bind the Anglo-Saxons together.

THERE ARE THREE METHODS BY WHICH A UNION MAY BE ESTABLISHED:

By Absorption Of All Into One Nation

First, by uniting all the English and Americans into one nation. At the present time such a course is absolutely impracticable, for reasons so weighty and obvious that they need not be mentioned.[49] What the far future will develop I shall not now seek to foretell; I can only raise the curtain high enough to enable us to behold our near destiny. But the necessities of the English-speaking people may yet drive them into one nation, and from such a possibility they need not shrink. The entire English-speaking races might be happily united under a *constitutional monarchy*, or a *republican federative government*. Many worse things could happen to them in their national life than their consolidation into one nation. But as there is nothing in existing conditions which requires such a radical and revolutionary step, I regard its discussion as quite useless. I allude to it merely to clear the way for more practical suggestions.[50]

By Establishing A Federation

The second means by which a permanent union could be created between Great Britain and her colonies, and the United States and her colonies and dependencies, would be by establishing a federation. A federation, however, is also impracticable. A federation is the union of several independent states for purposes of mutual interest, protection, and support; each state reserving the control of its own internal affairs, but surrendering to the federative council, or body, or executive, whichever may be chosen to exercise them, all powers necessary to enable the

[49] Still the author of *The Americanization of the World*, W. T. Stead, boldly advocates such a step.

[50] But the thought is not one which sees the light for the first time in this book. It was the dream of many English and Americans before the Revolution, as Mr. Lecky attests: "The maintenance of one free, industrial, and pacific empire, comprising the whole English race, holding the richest plains of Asia in subjection, blending all that was most venerable in an ancient civilisation with the redundant energies of a youthful society, and destined in a few generations to outstrip every competitor and acquire an indisputable ascendancy on the globe, may have been a dream, but it was at least a noble one, and there were Americans who were prepared to make any personal sacrifices rather than assist in destroying it." Mr. Lecky uses this language in eulogising the course of the Loyalists during the Revolution.— *History of England in the Eighteenth Century*, vol. iii., p. 418.

government thus created to deal with foreign or external questions, and to carry out the purposes for which the federation has been established.

The difficulty in establishing a federation is, that neither the United States nor England would be willing to surrender its national individuality and rank in the same degree of statehood as Canada, Australia, or one of the minor colonies or dependencies of either of the first-named countries. A federation places each independent state, politically at least, upon an equal footing, and the disparity of population, or territory (to say nothing of prestige) is too great to render such a plan practicable.[51]

By A Treaty—Regulating Their Conduct And Intercourse With Each Other

A third method of creating a union between these nations is by a treaty binding upon all of them, by which certain rules shall be established regulating their relations towards each other, but not to foreign nations. This I believe furnishes practical means of establishing a permanent and substantial understanding, *entente*, or union between the English-American people; and when I have used the terms "union," "alliance," and the like, in the preceding parts of this book, I mean that, whatever it may be called, it shall be created by a written instrument, and attested by a legal, constitutional, and binding treaty between all of the English and American powers and colonies.

The Reasons Existing Against The First Two, And In Favor Of The Last Method

By this method a union can be established without forming a federation—which means too much on the one side, in the surrender of position and individuality by the United States and England—while mere vague, indefinite expressions of sympathy and ephemeral good feeling, on the other, accomplish too little. It is too much to demand or expect a federation; while a mere moral *entente* falls short in effectiveness and practical result. We have already passed through the stage of an *entente* consisting of mutual good-will, interest, forbearance, and respect; we have a good and solid knowledge of each other, so that we are now ready to cement this feeling by measures which will bring us so close together as to be practically one people.

I therefore open a conservative method—a compromise between a federation and mere verbal expressions of good-will, which can be consummated by a treaty authorised by the people of the United States and by the Parliament of Great Britain, and by the peoples of all the colonies of both nations, and which shall embrace the following subjects:

First: The Dominion of Canada voluntarily to divide itself into such different states, geographically arranged, as its citizens desire, in proportion to population, and each state to be admitted as a full member of the American Union in accor-

---

[51] See in this connection Professor Freeman's *Greater Greece and Greater Britain*, Appendix, p. 105, where reference is made to an attempt more than fifteen years ago to establish a federation between Great Britain and her Colonies under the paradoxical title of "Imperial Federation."

dance with the conditions of the Constitution of the United States.

Second: To establish common citizenship between all the citizens of the United States and the British Empire.

Third: To establish absolute freedom of commercial intercourse and relations between the countries involved, to the same extent as that which exists between the different States constituting the United States of America.

Fourth: Great Britain and the United States to coin gold, silver, nickel, and copper money, not necessarily displaying the same devices or mottoes, but possessing the same money value, and interchangeable everywhere within the limits covered by the treaty; and to establish a uniform standard of weights and measures.

Fifth: To provide for a proper and satisfactory arbitration tribunal to decide all questions which may arise under the treaty.

I shall proceed to give in detail my reasons for each of these propositions. I am conscious that this general plan may be, in many of its details, susceptible to criticism. But it furnishes a basis for discussion and amendment. I give it as a whole. Mould it, shape it, until it is symmetrical, and its dimensions rise as sublime and majestic as the greatest monuments of ancient and modern liberty. Magna Charta and the Constitution of the United States were formed to establish, and have preserved, the principles of liberty, justice, and equality among the Anglo-Saxon race.

Let us, the descendants of the pioneers of this race, perpetuate and further extend our influence, power, and the political beatitudes which form our system of government, by uniting in a common brotherhood, and attested by a third monumental instrument which will further instinctively mark our progress as a people.

CHAPTER VII

THE SUBJECTS TO BE COVERED BY A TREATY

I. THE DOMINION OF CANADA TO BECOME A PART OF THE UNITED STATES OF AMERICA

I. The Dominion of Canada voluntarily to divide itself into different states, geographically arranged as its citizens desire, in proportion to population, and each state to be admitted as a full member of the American Union.

I approach this subject with the greatest diffidence, for, plainly as I perceive its necessity, I mistrust my ability to make clear to others the motives and causes which induce me to believe that the consolidation of Canada into our Republic is an indispensable condition to the establishment of a complete and permanent brotherhood between the Anglo-Saxon people. Canada a part of the United States by her free and voluntary act, generously and freely seconded by England, and graciously accepted by the United States, the Anglo-Saxon race *eo instanti* becomes a unit in sympathy, purpose, and progress.

With Canada a separate nation, as she is now, a real, lasting *entente* between the British Empire and the United States, is impossible.

"'T is true 't is pity; and pity 't is 't is true."

At the first blush I am sure to encounter reluctance and opposition on all sides—from the Canadians as well as the English and Americans. I meet at the outset sentiment and pride, two of the strongest and most invincible sentinels that guard the approach to human reason and judgment. As Mr. Lecky says: "The sentiment of nationality is one of the strongest and most respectable by which human beings are actuated. No other has produced a greater amount of heroism and self-sacrifice, and no other, when it has been seriously outraged, leaves behind it such enduring and such dangerous discontent."[52]

While the bond existing between England and Canada is sentimental and as "light as air," it creates a union between the two people "as strong as iron." Canada would never renounce England's formal sovereignty without her fullest and freest consent; and I believe England would exhaust the last drop of her blood to prevent a forcible annexation. Canadian sentiment and English pride stand ready to oppose the proposition. The United States, on the other hand, does not seek or want Canada to join the Union, and deep and strong opposition to such a course

---

[52] *History of England in the Eighteenth Century*, vol. ii., p. 50.

may also be encountered here. On the mere face of the question, therefore, annexation seems difficult and hard to accomplish. It should not be forced. It cannot be bought. Neither arms, money, nor commercial advantages can be of themselves sufficient potent factors to accomplish this end. It must come voluntarily: it must spring from the hearts of the people. It is well not to underestimate the difficulties of the proposition, and with that view I have gone beneath the surface in search of higher and nobler motives than those which ordinarily impel individual or national action. In this way only can sentiment be satisfied and pride placated. But it will be argued by some, ice must be broken to reach annexation; if all three parties interested must be converted to this view, why not, if it is to come at all, leave it to the "fulness of time," or, in other words, to processes entirely natural. As it now stands, say they, there is no impelling necessity, no heavy past experience of evils to force us together, as in the case of Scotland, and of our thirteen original States—no circumstances, on the other hand, that directly favour it.

But I ask the Canadians, the English, and the Americans, in all seriousness, When will the "fulness of time" occur? I assert that the fulness of time has been reached, and that the natural processes have matured. They have ripened over night as the result of years being crowded into two events—the Spanish-American and the Boer Wars. These wars show us our weaknesses and our strength.

The Anglo-Saxons, to be impregnable, must be united. I shudder to draw the reverse picture. Shall we wait until a dispute occurs between us? Shall we fold our arms until a war breaks out, and reveals through its lurid light our real relation to each other? Thucydides says: "In peace and prosperity both states and individuals are actuated by higher motives, because they do not fall under the dominion of *imperious necessities.*"[53] If we wait until our necessities tell us that we belong to one family and should be confederated together, who can divine the conditions and inequalities which will result? Can we not now, therefore, look the situation fully and candidly in the face, and decide calmly and dispassionately in what our best interests consist?

I admit that the mere aggrandisement of the United States by the extension of her territory; the benefit to Canada by opening the door to material development and improved commercial privileges; the release of England from the heavy and unprofitable responsibility of defending Canada against attacks by the United States,—these are influences which, though none are more weighty and important, would not of themselves operate to produce annexation. *They must be combined with others, connected with the future welfare and progress of all the three powers involved.* We must all see and realise that our future onward march can only be successfully made together. Interest, in other words, must be combined with sentiment. In the great march towards civilisation we cannot take separate paths. The Anglo-Saxons must go together.

I take it for granted, therefore, that we truly believe the solidarity of the Anglo-Saxon races is the great desideratum of this century; and that although it may be more important to England than to the United States or Canada to hasten this result, yet all three are so bound up together that in the end they are vitally inter-

[53] *Thucydides* (Jowett), 2nd ed., vol. i., p. 242.

ested in bringing about a common understanding as quickly as circumstances will admit it.

The present relation which Canada and the United States and England bear to each other confirms this last view. England is the third party standing between Canada and the United States in the negotiation. What is her position? What are her interests? What position has she in the ultimate annexation of Canada? What should she do—aid or oppose annexation? I shall endeavour to answer these questions satisfactorily.

The present Dominion of Canada, consisting of the Provinces of Quebec, Nova Scotia, New Brunswick, Prince Edward Island, Ontario, Manitoba, British Columbia, and the other unorganised territories, was created by virtue of the Act of the Imperial Parliament of Great Britain, entitled "The British North American Act, 1867." This Statute practically constituted the Dominion of Canada an independent nation, subject only to the Imperial power of Great Britain as to its foreign relations. Since its passage the English Government exercises no more actual rule in the Dominion of Canada than it does in Chicago or New York; in fact, Canada can even maintain formidable tariffs to keep Great Britain out of her markets. I do not overlook the fact that Canadian co-operation, in men and money, may always be relied upon by the mother country in the time of her need, nor do I belittle the moral support which the Canadians will extend to her when required. Canada is a pure and shining jewel in her imperial crown.

Therefore she would undoubtedly make sacrifices in parting with Canada. But she could not retain Canada by force against the will of the latter; and she would not do so even if she could. While it is also true that a formal English representation is still kept up, the Dominion of Canada as a matter of fact, through a Governor-General, is now bound to Great Britain, notwithstanding the forms created by the Act of 1867, only by a mere sentimental tie—a bond of sympathy recently, by the Boer War, renewed and strengthened and now so strong that both Canada and Great Britain would probably exhaust themselves in endeavouring to maintain it if sought to be forcibly rent asunder. Such is the ligament which binds these two powers. Conquest *in such a case,* even in the event of war, is out of the question. If the Canadians were subdued by the Americans, God forbid that they should sink so low in the scale of generosity and national manhood as to forcibly annex them to their Government! And, if conquest will not avail, it requires something more than logic and selfish argument to dissolve such a tie. The particular sympathy which exists between Canada and the British Empire must be balanced by the future vital interests of the whole Anglo-Saxon people; and while mere selfish interests might not alone appeal to these three nations to agree voluntarily to annexation, the ultimate *safety, welfare, progress,* and *unity* of the whole Anglo-Saxon race should affect them when everything else might fail. Would the Canadians stand in the way of the accomplishment of such a mighty result? Would not England under such circumstances generously yield to a request of Canada for consent to annexation?

I shall endeavour to traverse the whole field of the discussion, and lay bare every view that can influence fair and honest judgment. As a matter of fact, the position of England, as she stands between Canada and the United States, is not an enviable one. She is liable any minute to be involved in a war with the latter power on account of the former, in whom she has not a great material interest, and from whom her people receive very little appreciable benefit. As a question of mere selfish policy, therefore, England has everything to gain by the annexation of Canada to the United States, and everything to lose by continuing to be her *formal* sovereign and her *actual* champion. It is true, that under the present relations, if unhappily a war should ever occur between England and the United States, England might worry the United States through Canada, but it is not too much to say that this worriment would be of short duration. Any misunderstanding between Canada and the United States, involving war, precipitates England in a bloody and ruinous contest with the United States, without having the slightest material interest in the issue. She would gain by being relieved of this immense burden of responsibility, which exists without any adequate *quid pro quo*, or corresponding advantage. What more trying position for England than the necessity of championing quarrels not of her own making, where both of the contending parties have claims upon her forbearance, and in a sphere where her powers and resources would have to be employed to the full, and then only wasted? There arises out of these conditions a question of grave import, whether any nation is justified, before its own people, in assuming such a burdensome relation. I do not argue the point, I merely ask the question—"Has England the right to spill the blood of her people and spend their money; should she involve the happiness and future of her citizens to maintain this purely sentimental tie?" Quite apart from all this, it is reasonably certain, judging from her conduct towards her other colonies, that if Canada should desire to disrupt the formal relations existing between herself and England, the latter power would acquiesce upon a simple request.

I pass, then, to the relations between Canada and the United States accruing out of England's position. In the event of a dispute between England and the United States, Canada, although perfectly disinterested in the quarrel, is liable to be drawn into a war, because she happens to have a formal relation with England, and acknowledges that power as sovereign. The first shock of a war between England and the United States would be felt by Canada. Her condition is paradoxical; it creates a dilemma; it evolves a situation most remarkable and striking. England can be forced into a war because of her empty and hollow sovereignty over Canada; Canada is subject to destruction because she officially acknowledges England's sovereignty. Either nation is liable to invasion and devastation, if not ruin, because of formal ties. If the power of England were to decline and wane,—which Heaven forbid!—what would be the future of Canada? Isolated from England, where could she turn, except to the one contiguous power of the United States, and perhaps under circumstances far less pleasant than those which would accompany a voluntary union. These are serious aspects of the question. Standing alone, notwithstanding their importance, these considerations might not be overpowering, but if the situation described above can be dissipated by a free, voluntary, honourable, and wholesome alliance, is it not for the advantage of all that it be accomplished, thereby removing for all time the serious consequences which may at any moment arise from these formal and anomalous conditions? Remove the cause and avoid the result.

But there are other views which must not be overlooked or disregarded. Canada is a friendly neighbour of the United States, but a fast-growing commercial rival. Separated as adjoining owners are from each other, by a mere partition, a division line, and capable of walking upon the other's territory at will, the results of this physical contiguity are easily foretold. Jealousies, rivalries, encroachments upon each other, and grievances fast piling up between them, are liable to set the feelings and passions of their people afire by the most insignificant discord or incident. But why cannot we live together as Christian neighbours and friends, striving to reach a common goal, and attending to our own affairs? So far as mere physical area is concerned, there is undoubtedly room for two Anglo-Saxon nations to exist separately and independently upon this continent, working out their own destinies in their own way, and not only undisturbed, but aided and encouraged by each other. Moreover, as Canada is the weaker nation, the Americans should treat her not only fairly, but generously. I think that this spirit predominates among the greater portion of the people of the United States to-day. I do not believe there are any considerable number of Americans anxious to have Canada become a member of their political household, except by her free and unqualified consent. I know there are only a few who would think of force or purchase to consummate that result. But, on the other hand, there are many Canadians and Americans who would welcome annexation if it could be brought about graciously and naturally. If Canada and the United States could exist as independent nations; if their political orbits (in other words their laws of movement) were fixed externally apart; if by commercial treaties they would open to each other free and unrestricted trade; if their citizens would intermingle not as jealous rivals and strangers, but as fair competitors and friends, their international existence would be ideal. As long as we are separated, I insist that decency and good manners should teach us to treat Canada as a friend and neighbour. We should study the rights and duties of *meum et tuum*. And no matter what eventually becomes of the proposition here suggested, we should be generous and broad in our treatment of her. But is it safe to expect all this? Is it human nature? Will not self-interest and temporary advantage dominate our behaviour when the critical moment comes? I appeal to the good sense and judgment of the Anglo-Saxon people; I point to all history to answer these questions. I interject no opinion of my own, except so far as it is founded upon the actions of states and nations situated similarly to the United States and Canada. What has been the result? If mutual consent has not brought them together, has not union been accomplished by force? It would have been ideal for the original thirteen States to have existed as independent nations, developing and extending themselves into the highest stages of civilisation; but aside from the immediate necessity which drove them into a federation, how long could they have existed apart as independent states? The cities of Greece remained separate and independent for ages, but they at length succumbed, vainly striving to combine when combination was too late. And what was their condition before this? Were they not constantly at war with each other? Are not some of our most glowing illustrations of the efficiency and soundness of confederate governments drawn from the history of Grecian cities; and is not the language of Professor Freeman, in speaking of these Greek cities, most strikingly and forcibly applicable to Canada and the United States?

"But there is a far greater evil inherent in a system of separate free cities, an evil which becomes only more intense as they attain a higher degree of greatness and glory. (And I might add commercial rivalry.) This is the constant state of war which is almost sure to be the result. When each town is perfectly independent and sovereign, acknowledging no superior upon earth, multitudes of disputes, which in a great monarchy or a federal republic, may be decided by peaceful tribunals, can be settled by nothing but an appeal to the sword. The thousand causes which involve large neighbouring states in warfare all exist, and all are endowed with tenfold force in the case of independent city commonwealths. Border disputes, commercial jealousies, wrongs done to individual citizens, the mere vague dislike which turns a neighbour into a natural enemy, all exist, and that in a form condensed and intensified by the very minuteness of the scene on which they have to act. A rival nation is, to all but the inhabitants of a narrow strip of frontier, a mere matter of hearsay: but a rival whose dwelling-place is within sight of the city gates quickly grows into an enemy who can be seen and felt. The highest point which human hatred can reach has commonly been found in the local antipathies between neighbouring cities.[54] ... The greatest work that orator or diplomat ever achieved was when Demosthenes induced the two cities to lay aside their differences and join in one common struggle for the defence of Greece against the Macedonian invader."[55]

Another authority develops the same views:

"Neighbouring nations are natural enemies of each other, unless their common weakness forces them to league in a confederate republic, and their constitution prevents the differences that neighbourhood occasions, extinguishing that secret jealousy which disposes all States to aggrandise themselves at the expense of their neighbours."

This sentence is quoted by Alexander Hamilton,[56]. in reference to which the latter adds this significant remark: "This passage at the same time points out the *evil* and suggests the *remedy*."

As long as we remain apart, are not tensions, discords, and differences imminent? And at some unexpected moment will not a fanatic, politician, or demagogue cast a brand into the fire of discussion, and then will we not have war? As Canada grows in her development, and increases in prosperity and population, will not these dangers become more likely and pressing?[57] I frankly and gladly

---

[54] Freeman, *History of Federal Government in Greece and Italy*, 2d ed., p. 42 *et seq.*

[55] *Ibid.*, p. 43.

[56] From "Principes des Negociacions," par l'Abbé de Mably, the *Federalist*, No. VI., Lodge's Ed., p. 32.

[57] As illustrating these views I quote from an interview published in the *New York Herald* of Sunday, June 15, 1902, with Sir Wilfrid Laurier, Prime Minister of Canada, before leaving for London, to attend the coronation ceremonies and the conference of Colonial Premiers, as follows: "The most important question just now, as affecting the relations and

admit that the chances of war between the United States and England are becoming less probable every day. The only existing bone of contention which might create war is Canada. There is no other question which cannot, and, I hope, will not be settled by agreement, or arbitration. With Canada annexed, and *a common citizenship established*, all causes for differences would be removed, and we would practically become one great nation, with one great purpose and a single ambition—to civilise mankind.

The disadvantages and evils which result to the three nations concerned from the present anomalous government of Canada are apparent and susceptible of much more elaboration than I have indulged in. I leave much to the imagination. Real harm may ensue from opening up these matters with too much detail. On the other hand, in searching for the advantages of union, we find all the natural causes which tend to and justify the consolidation of separate states present.

Contiguity of territory, the same race of people; the same language, literature, and laws; the same political and religious tendencies; the dominating necessities of commerce; self-protection, mutual interest, motives of peace and good-will—in fine, all those elements necessary to insure a prosperous and permanent political marriage. Almost every reason which operated upon the minds of the citizens of the original thirteen States to create the present federation is to be found in the case of Canada. She is naturally related to the United States; she is only artificially connected with England. In a commercial and material sense, the advantages of her annexation to the United States are potent. She would move forward with gigantic strides, opening, developing, and peopling her vast country. In separate States of the American Union, the Canadians would cultivate and guard their own destinies, just as the present States of the Union now do. The free and unrestricted admixture of the people of the different States of the American Union has been one of the causes of her vast progress. Break down the political paper barrier which now exists between Canadians and Americans, open the door between them so that each can pass in and out of the other's country, establish a free communion of persons and goods, and Canada would leap into a condition of progress and prosperity equal to that of our most envied and successful States. American capital, invention, and push would combine with Canadian ability, energy, and resources to reach the highest stage of individual and national development.

The road to great prosperity is now blocked by the mere form of a different citizenship, although we are really one people. We are standing idly looking at each other, relying upon forced, strained, and unnatural efforts to build up commercial relations, when we have it in our power, by the stroke of a pen, as it were, to reach the goal of business, fortune, and success.

Cannot the Canadians learn an important lesson from a study of the history of Scotland? I do not mean to assert that there is a perfect historical parallel, but

---

friendly feeling existing between Canada and the United States, is the Alaska boundary question. This situation is full of danger, and all that is required to precipitate a disgraceful conflict is the discovery of gold in the disputed territory." This difficulty has happily been arranged by treaty and the question left to six arbitrators, but at the present writing Canada newspapers are urging strenuous objections against two of the American arbitrators.

there are significant events connected with that history which certainly bear upon this discussion. Causes which led to the merger into one of the different Saxon kingdoms, gradually to the annexation of Wales, and finally to the absorption of the Palatinates, had long been working toward similar results in both England and Scotland. The wisest statesmen in these two countries deplored those miseries which, till they ceased to be divided, each inflicted on the other. The Scots, though uncertain, intractable, and passionately jealous of their national liberties, again and again allowed the question to approach the edge of solution.[58] In fact, the union of Scotland and England was agitated in different forms for many hundred years before it was accomplished, with the most lamentable consequences in the interim, to say nothing of the policy of Edward I., and the aspirations and efforts of Henry VIII. to achieve that result after the marriage of his sister, Margaret, with James IV. of Scotland. The supreme effort of King James I., in 1606, to effect a union between the two kingdoms, when the matter was brought before Parliament, and the extraordinary zeal shown by Sir Francis Bacon in support thereof, are well known. "Swayed merely by the vulgar motive of national antipathy," as Hume puts it,[59] the attempt was defeated, and one hundred years elapsed before the important event was consummated. Upon its final accomplishment, Scotland gave up many rights and accepted a representation inadequate and small in comparison to her population, much to the nation's chagrin and loss; but everybody now admits that it was a wise and eminently necessary step for her future prosperity. If it had not been accomplished[60] there would have been a renewal of national wars and border feuds, the cost of which the two kingdoms could never have endured, and at a hazard of ultimate conquest, which, with all her pride and bravery, the experience of the last generation had shown to be no impossible result of the contest.

I wish, also, to recall the important fact, that Canada was originally embraced in the plan of the American Republic, as provided in the Articles of Confederation (XI.) as follows:

"Canada acceding to this Confederation, and joining in the measures of the United States, shall be admitted into, and entitled to all the advantages of, this Union, but *no other colony shall be admitted into the same unless such admission be agreed to by nine States.*"

The door was left wide open for her admission, but she did not avail herself of the privilege to enter. Her actual reason for not accepting an offer which placed her on a par with the most prosperous colonies of England, I cannot satisfactorily discover. I can guess, but speculation upon this point answers no practical purpose. The anomalous fact is, however, recorded that while the French Canadians were combating American Independence, the French nation was aiding the Americans to attain it. It is important to keep in sight that it was the opinion of the founders of our Government that geographically, commercially, and naturally, Canada belonged to the same sphere of political life in which they revolved. Indeed it requires no strained or artificial argument to show that Canada naturally

[58] Froude's *History of England*, vol. vii.. p. 101.
[59] Hume's *History of England*, vol. iv., p. 251.
[60] See Hallam's *Const. Hist. of England*, vol. iii., p. 325.

belongs to the Union; just as naturally as the Union belongs to Canada.

Goldwin Smith's remarks are pertinent in this connection[61]:

"Yet there is no reason why the union of the two sections of the English-speaking people on this continent should not be as free, as equal, and as honourable as the union of England and Scotland. . . . When the Anglo-Saxons of England and those of Scotland were reunited they had been many centuries apart; those of the United States and Canada have been separated for one century only. The Anglo-Saxons of England and Scotland had the memory of many wars to estrange them. . . . That a union of Canada with the American Commonwealth, like that into which Scotland entered with England, would in itself be attended with great advantages, cannot be questioned, whatever may be the considerations on the other side, or the reasons for delay. It would give to the inhabitants of the whole continent as complete a security for peace and immunity from war taxation, as is likely to be attained by any community or group of communities on this side of the Millennium. Canadians, almost with one voice, say, that it would greatly raise the value of property in Canada; in other words, that it would bring with it a great increase of prosperity."

From time to time, sporadic attempts have been made by Canadians to force a sentiment in favour of annexation, but they have been abortive. In 1847, the American flag was hoisted on the Town Hall in Kingston, and in 1849 many prominent men in Montreal signed an annexation manifesto.[62] No widespread, overwhelming feeling in its favour, however, has ever been developed in Canada, or encouraged or countenanced by any considerable number of citizens of the United States; in fact, the latter have displayed a cold and almost unnatural indifference to the movement, which, under the circumstances, is remarkable. This apathy is largely due to the fact that the subject has never been considered as a serious, vital issue. It is now fully opened to us. That this annexation will come I have no doubt. How, when, and under what circumstances, I will not prophesy. I pray it may not come by force. If Canada does not feel that she can enter into political communion with the Americans upon terms of perfect equality, we have nothing to do but fold our arms and accept the situation. The event ought to come as a true and loving marriage, with a full volition on each side, inspired by the double sentiment of mutual respect and interest. There should not be a particle of force, or a scintilla of commercial bribery about it. Until this moment arrives we should be patient with each other. If sometimes we must quarrel, remember that we pretend and proclaim ourselves to be the most civilised and Christian people on the face of the earth, and therefore ought to settle our disputes in a spirit of broadness and equity, and agree with our adversary quickly. Above and beyond this, let the Americans always remember that Canada is the weaker nation, and that true Anglo-Saxon manhood requires that they should be generous to her, and give her the benefit of all doubt. The more magnanimous they are, the more tender in their treatment of Canada, the more quickly will come the desired event—a complete and happy

[61] *Canada and the Canadian Question*, p. 267 *et seq.*

[62] "Commercial Relations between Canada and the United States," by Robert Mc-Connell, *Canadian Magazine*, January, 1889.

union. Nothing will postpone its consummation so much as a narrow, bigoted policy towards her.

I will not assert that I have much faith in immediate annexation. I sincerely hope it may soon come. I fully believe in its eventuality. In the meantime I simply bring the question before Canadians, Americans, and Britons, but I cannot complete this sentence by adding, "Let nature take its course." This would mean that I thought events were not ripe; that the fruit was green and immature. Such is not my opinion. I believe every condition exists which makes the event feasible. I fear postponement, because I am warned by history that men and nations have never yet learned to control their passions at times when they should be calm, just, and generous.

When one says, "Let nature take its course," he may also mean that in the ordinary course of affairs arms and force may be used, while the weapons should be those of love and agreement. But a time may come when the Canadians and Americans, suddenly imbued with a feeling of interest and sympathy, will voluntarily move towards each other, and become unified through circumstances which will make an ideal political marriage.

I recall that Lord Bacon advocated, in his own powerful and masterly way, the union of Scotland and England more than one hundred years before it was actually accomplished, and that history, reason, and argument were then disregarded and cast aside as so many straws.[63] But ideas survive. They cannot be destroyed. And Bacon's views eventually prevailed.

If I am called visionary; if my arguments are criticised as unsound; if my suggestions are stamped as inconclusive; if my results are laughed at, I shall find myself, or somebody else will find me, in most select and distinguished company; and certainly that will furnish some compensation for the time I am spending on this subject.

All I can do now is to sow a few seeds in this reluctant soil, and hope that at some time they may produce ripe and wholesome fruit. If my efforts are barren, other toilers will come in the same field of thought, and finally events, through one cause or another, will shape themselves into mature results, thus realising that which nature, destiny, self-interest, and national glory demand; the inhabitants of this North American continent will become one people, all Anglo-Saxon by birth or adoption—united in one free and prosperous government.

II.—COMMON CITIZENSHIP

I have now reached the crucial point of my subject: the *common citizenship*; the placing of all the members of the Anglo-Saxon race on a political equality; conferring upon, them equal civic rights in the countries and colonies which they govern, making an Englishman a citizen of the United States and an American a citizen of England. By a single stroke of parliamentary and constitutional legislation the individuals composing the Anglo-Saxon race would enjoy common political rights, and, in fact and deed, become members of the same political family. This would

[63] "Tracts Relating to Scotland," Lord Bacon's *Works*, vol. v., edited by Basil Montagu.

resemble the important edict of Antoninus Caracalla, which communicated to all the free inhabitants of the Roman Empire, the name and privileges of Roman citizens. Professor Mommsen[64] says:

"When a stranger was by resolution of the community adopted into the circle of the burgesses, he might surrender his previous citizenship, in which case he passed wholly into the new community; but he might also combine his former citizenship with that which had just been granted to him. Such was the primitive custom, and such it always remained in Hellas, where in later ages the same person not infrequently held the freedom of several communities at the same time."

There would be no force or compunction in this common citizenship. The volition to embrace temporarily or permanently a citizenship in any other English-speaking country would rest with each individual. The barrier raised by the naturalisation laws would be removed, and the citizens of any English or American country could pass to and fro as freely as a person can move from one room to another, invested with full civic rights wherever they should happen to be. An Englishman under the American flag would be an American; an American under the English flag would be an Englishman. A citizen of Great Britain visiting the United States would, upon landing, become *eo instanti* a citizen of the United States, *pro hac vice*, pending the duration of his visit. He would become a citizen of the United States with all the privileges and immunities of such citizenship, and also a citizen of the individual State in which he resides during his sojourn, subject, of course, to the municipal laws and regulations of each State applicable to all citizens in respect to length of residence and domicile; and, *per contra*, a citizen of the United States visiting Great Britain, Ireland, or Australia would, in like manner, and to the same extent, become a citizen of England, Ireland, or Australia, with all necessary sequences flowing from citizenship. Under this rule, therefore, an Englishman visiting New York would have the right to vote at a presidential or congressional election, subject, of course, to the restrictions as to residence applicable to all citizens of the United States, such as residing in the State or Congressional district for a fixed period of time anterior to the election.

In other words, without any actual or formal expatriation of his own country on the one side, or preliminary probation, quarantine, or naturalisation on the other, he would instantly, upon landing in the United States, by force of law become a citizen of the United States, subject to Federal and State restrictions, applicable to all citizens in general. The proposition means, in effect, an abrogation of the naturalisation laws of each country in favor of the Anglo-Saxon people.

A citizen of Australia, visiting New York, would, upon landing, become a citizen of the United States as long as he chose to reside there; and a citizen of the United States visiting Melbourne, would, in like manner, become a citizen of Australia pending his sojourn in that country. This may be called common or reciprocal citizenship. The Greeks termed it "Isopolity," of which more hereafter.

I shall elaborate still further the effects of common citizenship. For example, if this rule were adopted, a New York lawyer would be entitled to practise law in En-

---

[64] *History of Rome*, vol. i., p. 88, Dickens's edition, 1894.

gland, as solicitor or barrister, subject to the regulations laid down in this respect for British subjects; it would entitle him to enter Parliament, and, in fine, to enjoy the emoluments, ranks, and honours of the highest English offices, except so far as he is restrained by the Constitution of the United States, which would necessarily be altered to conform to the principles of the treaty in question.

On the other hand, a citizen of Dublin, *eo instanti*: upon landing in New York, would be entitled to all the prerogatives of American citizenship, and to all the offices and honours which that relation may lead to, save that of President, which can only be enjoyed by a native-born citizen of the United States. But without an amendment to the Constitution of the United States, a citizen of Great Britain, temporarily enjoying the rights of American citizenship, as proposed, could not immediately become a member of Congress, for by Subdivision 2 of Section 2, Article I. of the Constitution of the United States, it is provided that:

"No person shall be a representative who shall not have attained the age of twenty-five years, and have been seven years a citizen of the United States, and who shall not, when elected, be an inhabitant of the State in which he shall be chosen";

and by Subdivision 3, of Section 3, of the same Article, it is also declared that:

"No person shall be a Senator who shall not have attained to the age of thirty years and been nine years a citizen of the United States, and who shall not, when elected, be an inhabitant of that State for which he shall be chosen."

While the English Parliament, by a single act, could authorise a treaty which would carry into effect all the propositions above stated, to make the benefits of common citizenship reciprocal and equal it would be necessary on our side to amend the Constitution of the United States.

If the principle was acquiesced in, the lawyers would soon put these suggestions into practical shape.

There are two classes of rights which would follow the establishment of common citizenship, viz., civil and political.

The civil rights, *inter alia*, would be these:

1. An Isopolite would enjoy the same rights to real estate as a native-born citizen, such as buying, selling, trading in, or disposing of the same by will; and the slender thread and fragment of the alien laws still remaining in the United States, so far as they apply to citizens whose respective Governments are parties to the treaty, would necessarily disappear.

2. He would possess the same commercial rights and privileges of business as a native-born citizen.

3. He would enjoy the same material rights and privileges and be subject to the same limitations and duties as pertain to native-born citizens.

His political rights, among others, would be:

1. He would be entitled to vote at all Federal elections.

2. The right to vote at all State, county, or municipal elections, precisely the same as citizens of one of the States of the United States.

But while enjoying the same rights, he would be under the same disabilities, and be subject to the performance of the same duties as a citizen of the United States, as, for instance, to pay taxes, and to perform military or jury duty. If war should unhappily arise between the two nations, it must be admitted that all these rights would be rent asunder. *Inter armes silent leges.* But would not common citizenship be a most effectual barrier against war? And with Canada in the American Union, would not war, or even ugly disputes, be remote possibilities?

The principle of common citizenship is not novel; on the contrary, it is very ancient. Something like it existed in the Grecian states, which, in establishing a federal union among themselves, interchanged civic rights comprehended by the Greek word "Isopolity," There was also "Sympolity," which meant in effect the protection which a larger or stronger State gave to a smaller or weaker one,

In the "Byzantine Decree,"[65] it is *inter alia* provided:

"It is resolved by the people of the Byzantium and Perin thus to grant unto the Athenians the right of inter-marriage, citizenship, purchase of land and houses, the first seat at the games, first admission to the Council and People after the Sacrifices, and exemption from all public services to such as wish to reside in the City," and this because "they succoured us . . . and rescued us from grievous perils and preserved our hereditary constitution, our laws, and sepulchres,'"

"Isopolity," according to Niebuhr,[66] was a relation entered into by treaty between *two perfectly equal and independent cities*, mutually securing all those privileges to their citizens which a resident alien could not exercise at all, or only through the medium of a guardian; the rights of intermarriage, of purchasing landed property, of making contracts of every kind, of suing and being sued in person, of being exempted from taxes where citizens were so; and also partaking in sacrifices and festivals,

The *Cosmos*[67] is allowed to enter the senate house of the allied city that he may be able to propound the business of his state there; and as a mark of honour he has a seat in the popular assembly by the side of the magistracy, but without a vote.

The persons who enjoyed "Isopolity" were called "Isopolites."

This idea of Isopolity existed in some essential features among the Romans, for "between the Romans and Latins, and between the Romans and Caerites there existed this arrangement: that any citizen of the one state who wished to settle in the other, might, forthwith, be able to exercise there the rights of a citizen."[68]

The other relation, known as "Sympolity," subsisted between Rome and its

[65] Fully set forth in Demosthenes's Oration on the Crown, Bohn's *Classical Library*, p. 39.

[66] *History of Rome*, vol. ii., p. 51.

[67] *Ibid.*, p. 52.

[68] Niebuhr's Lecture on the History of Rome, vol. i., p. 125.

municipia: it was the connection of one place with another on a footing of inequality; the citizens of the subordinate state had not the same rights as those of the chief state, their advantage consisting in the close alliance with a powerful head, for protection, but they had no share in the election of magistrates (*civitas sine suffragio*), and the relation was altogether one-sided. Isopolite states, on the other hand, generally stood to each other in a relation of perfect equality, and were quite independent in their transactions with foreign countries.[69]

The Greeks learned the lesson too late in their national experience of the evils of *political isolation where nature intended there should be no isolation*. The one idea in which that wonderful people were deficient was political unity. Each city was a separate entity and proud of being such. The dividing causes were many and strong. Isopolity and the like were indications of an underlying sense of a better principle.

The great Pericles caused a law to be passed restricting the citizenship to those only whose parents were both Athenian—a law which afterwards he sought to have repealed so far as to exempt a son of his own.[70]

When foreigners became frequent in Athens, a public vote of the people was necessary, in each instance, to bestow citizenship. If that could not be obtained, some form of evasion of the law was resorted to.[71]

The policy of the Greeks in the above respects was in direct contrast to that of the Romans. When their dominion became assured, the latter welcomed into their bosom all allies and conquered peoples. The Greeks, it is true, when it was too late, driven by necessity, formed the Achaian League, which would have been real and efficacious, had not the power of Macedonia, against which it was first directed, proved too strong for the liberties of their country.

These pages of classic history have not escaped the attention of modern scholars and publicists, and I am not alone in seeking to apply ancient examples to existing conditions.

Professor Freeman[72] uttered a hope in 1885 that some day *common citizenship* would be established between the English-speaking nations.

"I have often dreamed that something like the Greek συμπολιτεία a power in the citizens in each country of taking up the citizenship of the other at pleasure, might not be beyond hope, but I have never ventured even to dream of more than that. It is our bad luck at present that there are only two independent English nations, two English nations which parted in anger, and neither of which has quite got over the unpleasant circumstances of parting."

And the same proposition of a common citizenship was advocated by Professor Dicey in 1897.[73] He stated that his

[69] Niebuhr's Lectures on Ethnography and Geography, vol. i., p. 141.
[70] *Vide* Plutarch's, *Pericles.*
[71] Grote, vol. iv., p. 186.
[72] Freeman's *Greater Greece and Greater Britain*, Appendix, p. 142.
[73] *Contemporary Review*, April, 1897.

"aim is to establish the possibility and advocate the policy of instituting a common citizenship for all Englishmen and Americans. My proposal is summarily this: That England and the United States should, by concurrent and appropriate legislation, create such a common citizenship, or, to put the matter in a more concrete and therefore in a more intelligible form, that an act of the Imperial Parliament should make every citizen of the United States, during the continuance of peace between England and America, a British subject, and that simultaneously an Act of Congress should make every British subject, during the continuance of such peace, a citizen of the United States."[74]

Mr. Bryce also suggested the same course[75]: "There are things which may be done at once to cement and perpetuate the good relations which happily prevail. . . *such as the recognition of a common citizenship, securing to the citizens of each in the country of the other certain rights not enjoyed by other foreigners.*"

While common citizenship would not affect in the least the political form or substance of the government of either country, the result of its adoption would practically make the English-speaking people, so far as the outside world is concerned, one nation, inspired by one great, noble purpose. And the ebb and flow of citizens from one country to the other could not fail to be beneficial in its influence upon the internal and external policy of each.

It will have been observed that in what I have heretofore said I have carefully eschewed the use of the word "alliance," This word conveys the impression of a written or defined compact between separate nations for an offensive or defensive purpose, as, for example, the "Triple Alliance," the "Franco-Russian Alliance." I wish to exclude utterly such an idea and keep it altogether out of view. Nothing is more distasteful to my feelings or farther from my thoughts than an alliance of the Anglo-Saxon race to browbeat or bully the world. While the suggestions I make must necessarily be carried into effect by a preliminary treaty, and while incidentally the contracting parties will be benefited, its great object is to establish and maintain universal peace. It seeks to unite the people.

If Canada becomes a part of the United States, the Canadians can possess all the rights of English citizenship when they chose to seek them by visiting any of the countries embraced in the British Empire—a privilege which they do not now enjoy. And *vice versa*, Englishmen can become citizens of any of the Canadian Provinces by simply landing on their soil. Englishmen and Canadians are now, inconsistently enough, political strangers to each other, but by an instantaneous operation of law they can, by their own volition, become fellow-citizens.

And will not the alleged grievances of the Irish roll away and disappear, like the burdens of Christian, in the Slough of Despond, before common citizenship? Will not the whole Anglo-Saxon race be practically united for the propagation

---

[74] This learned author subsequently lamented (*Atlantic Monthly*, October, 1898), that his proposal "fell flat. It was inopportune. It excited no attention in England, though it brought me a few friendly letters from the United States. But the tone of my correspondence was not encouraging."

[75] *Atlantic Monthly*, July, 1898.

of peace and civilisation? Will not the effect of common citizenship be to establish and enforce common rules of liberty and equality if, and where, they do not now already exist? Maintaining intact the peculiar governments which they now individually enjoy, will not the citizens of each feel that they are henceforth all interested in the welfare and glory of the whole race, and in the development of a common purpose? Will not a generous rivalry stimulate each to outdo the other in the breadth and liberality of their laws?

I shall say a word, in this connection, on the general subject of naturalisation laws, the abrogation of which I recommend in favour of our own kinsmen. A most superficial inspection of the history of the world will show that every nation has guarded from motives of pride, jealousy, or fear, the privilege of citizenship. The general policy has been to confine it to those born and bred on the soil, and not to permit the outside world, or foreigners, to become members of the State. Exceptions were necessarily made to this universal rule, but they were rare. A nation, in respect to citizenship, was looked upon as a family, and strangers were not admitted to the fold. These observations are not simply applicable to ancient States, but the same rule existed, and exists, in modern governments.

It is a fact worthy to be chronicled to its credit, that the United States was the first nation to throw open its doors to foreigners, and invite all persons to become members of its political family. Our ancestors settled in North America to establish and perpetuate civil and religious liberty, and all who were in search of these blessings and new homes were welcomed to its hospitable shores. Instead of being jealous of our citizenship, we were delighted to welcome all classes to our country, and to confer upon them full and equal civic rights. We wanted company, and our newly arrived guests shared to the full in everything we could consistently give in property and citizenship.

Behold the results! They are seen to-day in our social life. Wherever we have a place, a foreigner can find a cheery and sincere welcome. This custom, coeval with our national birth, has grown and developed until the Americans are acclaimed the most hospitable people on the face of the earth. None are equal to them as hosts. After our independence, there was an apprehension that foreigners might come here, and, with evil intent, propagate principles contrary to our political tenets. Accordingly, in the Constitution, Congress was given the power to make uniform naturalisation laws. Under this authority, the first Naturalisation Act was passed early in the nineteenth century. A quarantine was established to enable the foreigner to acquire our language and to become accustomed to our Government. Having passed the necessary probation, the naturalised foreigner is admitted to the fullest rank of citizenship, and there is no office or honour closed to him save one — the Presidency of the United States. Compare our policy, in this respect, with that of other nations, to see whether my eulogy is deserved.

We come, now, to solve the problem of a common citizenship for every member of the Anglo-Saxon race. Who but the American people can make such a proposition? Who but we are entitled to lead in such a movement? Where should such an invitation come from, but from the United States of America, and to whom should it be extended but to the members of our own family — to Englishmen,

Irishmen, Scotchmen, and Australians?

What are the objections to a curtailment, or an abolition, of the naturalisation laws, so far as the English-speaking people are concerned? This is practically all that is meant by common citizenship. Is it essential, or necessary, to the maintenance of any principle or policy of our Government, or of national safety, *that there should be a probation of five years, before an Irishman, or an Englishman, could become a citizen of the Republic of the United States of America*? I propound the same question to the English in favour of the Americans.

What was the object sought to be accomplished by the naturalisation laws? To establish and compel a probation while the immigrating foreigner was learning to speak our language, and becoming familiarised with the form of our Government. In these enlightened days, when almost every member of the Anglo-Saxon race can speak, read, and write English, is this limit of five years any longer efficacious or necessary? In the early days of our Republic, as can be seen by a perusal of the debates in the Constitutional Convention, much anxiety was felt and expressed upon the subject of admitting foreigners to citizenship. It was thought they would bring into our midst and propagate political ideas quite foreign and antagonistic to the principles of a republic, and hence were adopted the restrictions of seven and nine years in the Constitution, relating to the election of foreigners to the House of Representatives and to the Senate. But these influences are now effectually guarded against by virtue of the overwhelming domination of American-born subjects; and it is very doubtful whether any of the reasons which led to the adoption of a five years' residence preliminary to citizenship now exist. *Cessat ratione cessat lex.* Open wide our doors to the Anglo-Saxon race, whether they come from England, Ireland, Australia, or New Zealand. Welcome them not as aliens, but as political brothers and fellow-citizens.

I do not overlook the fact that there is an existing, not to say a strong, sentiment in the United States against foreign immigration. This feeling is based upon the necessity of protecting American labour. It is thought by some that the country, great and capacious as it is, is already overcrowded, and that, for a few years at least, until further development of its resources are made, and new fields of business, commerce, agriculture, and labour are opened, immigration should be curtailed, suspended, or even prohibited. If this objection had any relevancy to the present discussion, it is squarely answered by the fact that it has never been used to prevent the inflow of the *English-speaking people*. The sentiment against further immigration, or restricted immigration, is not, if I understand the subject correctly, aimed against those immigrants who come from English-speaking countries. No one, so far as I can learn, has raised his voice against this class of immigrants becoming citizens of the United States under proper conditions. The objection is especially directed against the Chinese, who might, if any encouragement were given them, no matter how slight, overrun the country and soon swamp the labouring classes—an eventuality which should be guarded against. In this respect it is unnecessary to advocate the removal of any of the barriers which now exist.

I admit, also, that the same feeling, but in a milder form, exists against a class of foreigners who do not speak the English language. But as to the English-speaking races, if the citizens of the United States are admitted to a common citizenship in Great Britain and her colonies, I cannot conceive why we on this side should hesitate to grant a reciprocal privilege. Do we not all instinctively feel the difference? Mongolians and foreigners of other nationalities in the one case; English, Americans, Scotch, and Irish in the other—nature draws the line for us.

Again, if Canada becomes an integral part of our Republican system, her vast and comparatively unexplored soil will at once be opened to the energy and activity of American skill, genius, and labour, and superfluous immigrants to the United States would be welcomed there, and soon absorbed in her vast territory. On the whole, I do not think the United States or Canada, perhaps the two nations more particularly interested in the subject, could suffer any disadvantage by removing, at a single stroke, all barriers which now prevent the citizens of England, Scotland, and Ireland, and all the other English-speaking colonies, from becoming citizens, *pro hac vice*, of these countries, instantly upon the adoption of a common citizenship law. After all, as I have said, the whole question resolves itself into a conditional or limited curtailment of the naturalisation laws. These have never been uniform; but have been fluctuating and capricious—adapted to meet existing conditions.

The laxity which has existed in the enforcement of these naturalisation laws is notorious, and has enabled all individuals so disposed to become members of our Republic by open evasion. The applications for citizenship now mainly come from the non-English-speaking people. The number of English-speaking immigrants is growing less every year, and Ireland and England will soon be drained. It is time this human current should be turned. There should be an ebb and flow between the English-speaking countries.

Another objection may be that the inauguration of common citizenship would open the door to fraudulent voting, by bringing hordes of people to this country on the eve of national, state, or municipal elections, to corrupt our ballot. There is, however, no force in this objection, because under the rules applicable to citizens of the United States, a voter must reside in the State where he casts his vote at least one year, and in the election district for a period ranging from thirty days to four months previous to the election. It is not probable that any political party or organisation could control a sufficient amount of money or exercise a strong enough influence upon immigrants by "colonisation," to control a question of national, state, or municipal importance. It is, moreover, a sword that cuts both ways, and affects all the countries involved, because what could be done in New York would be equally easy in London, Dublin, or in any of the colonies where an election might be held.

But strenuous objection might be urged by foreigners to the doctrine of a common citizenship embracing only the citizens and subjects of the English-speaking countries. Is it just and right to discriminate against non-English-speaking nations—against Russians, Germans, French, Italians, Spanish, and Austrians, who have contributed so largely to our population and to the development of our national resources? The obvious answer is, that we cannot consult foreigners, or foreign nations, in shaping the policy of our Government. It does not become them to say what the British Empire or the United States shall do in the establishment of relations with each other. These foreigners are attracted to *our* shores by the allurements of our political institutions and the prospects of fortune and success. Welcome and receive them all under proper restrictions; but let them have nothing to do with our Government until they become citizens thereof.

In the next place, it does not lie in the mouth of any foreign nation to object to any treaty which the United States and Great Britain may choose to make. When nations enter into treaties, there is no principle of international or natural law, or justice, which requires the contracting parties to consult foreign nations as to the terms and conditions of the contract. Each nation is a free agent, possessing absolute liberty and power to enter into any alliance which is deemed to be for its best interests, security, or progress, subject only to an arraignment before the high bar of a general public opinion where treaties and alliances are discussed upon the broad principles of truth and justice. It would no more lie in the mouth of Austria, Germany, or Italy, to find fault with a treaty made between Great Britain and the United States, adopting a common citizenship, as explained above, than it would be tolerated that Great Britain or the United States should object to the triple alliance which was made between Austria, Italy, and Germany, by Bismarck at the conclusion of the Franco-Prussian War for their mutual protection and support. When nations are entering into alliances they do not call into their councils foreign powers not directly concerned in the compact. But I do not rest the discussion upon any narrow or technical basis.

A treaty between Great Britain and the United States upon the lines heretofore indicated, is absolutely sustainable in the forum of conscience and justice, and it is an ample answer to any criticism which might be made of it, by a foreign power, to show that the basis of the treaty is self-preservation and interest, quite irrespective of that other unanswerable ground in international discussion, viz., that the aim and object of the treaty is the maintenance of universal peace.

Lastly, if there was any real and substantial objection to such a treaty on the ground that foreigners were excepted from the privileges of common citizenship, it might be provided that all such could immediately become English-American citizens, when they declared their intention to establish a permanent home in either Great Britain, the United States, Canada, Australia, or any of the colonies embraced in the treaty, *and were able to speak, read, and write the English language.* To this extent our naturalisation laws might be modified in favour of foreigners.

As one of the aims of this alliance would be to offer a home and citizenship to all persons who desired to embrace an English-American Nationality, there could be no objection to opening wide the doors to a class of immigrants such as those just referred to. This exception would be politic, and agreeable to one of the ultimate designs and motives of the treaty, viz., the propagation of the English language, as it would both operate as an incentive to induce foreigners to study and acquire the same, and fit themselves for eventual English-American citizenship. If the immigrants did not bring themselves within these conditions, there would seem to be no reason why the old laws of naturalisation should not be kept in full force.

The effect and result of a common citizenship in the English-speaking countries would be great and far reaching. To-day, the assertion, "I am an American," or, "I am an Englishman," is a passport securing safety and respect of person and property everywhere within the four quarters of the globe. How incomparably greater, more forcible, and striking the assertion would be, if a common citizenship were established such as I have above suggested! How talismanic such an utterance! In his oration against Verres, with what force and pride did Cicero dwell upon the magical power and effect of the words, "I am a Roman citizen"[76]

Men of no means, he said, holding no office or station in public or private life, poor or friendless, at sea, or in places where they were neither known to men among whom they had arrived, or able to find people to vouch for them, by uttering the mere phrase "I am a Roman," received protection from the laws, and shared the rights of hospitality to an extent not common to the citizens of other nations.

Besides, common citizenship would tend to restore the office of a citizen to its high and elevated sphere. It would produce "fitness," which, after all, is the quality to be sought for in the true citizen. While in times of war or dispute, the pride of country is fully aroused and exercises a marked influence upon its citizens, yet in the intervals of peace the real duties of citizenship are overlooked or disregarded. Shall we recall what these duties are, and the nature of the office of a citizen? *In most respects* this *office* is the *highest* that exists in any civilised government. Why? Because the government is established for his benefit. All the officers of the government are the agents of the citizens. The government is made for man, not man for the government, as Mr. Webster said. Public officers are trustees for the citizens, who are the *cestuis que trustent* — the beneficiaries. An individual born in a country becomes, so to speak, a citizen thereof by operation of law. There is no ceremony of investiture-no signing of a constitution — no oath — nothing to acquaint him with his duties, or to impress upon him the full measure of his responsibility. He becomes a citizen so naturally and imperceptibly that he often belittles the office, or fails to see its importance, or to understand the full measure and magnitude of his rights and duties. In a representative government the citizen surrenders his office to a representative and is removed far from the scenes of official action. He only participates in the government of the state, and in the making of laws, by proxy. In this respect the difference between a true democracy and a federated republic or constitutional monarchy is manifest. In the former, the citizens all actively participate in the making of laws; in the latter they are generally absent when legislation is enacted, and only appear by their representative. In a true democracy each citizen must take an active interest in every question that arises, because he is present and participating in all political discussions; in a federal republic, he knows very little of what is transpiring, for he has transferred his duties to a representative. In the former case the importance and responsibilities of citizenship are vividly impressed upon the democrat; in the latter these duties are unknown or neglected, and the burden thrown upon the proxy. The closer citizens are brought to legislation, the better government there will be. Do we not notice

---

[76] *Cicero's Orations*, vol. i., Bohn's Ed., p. 534 *et seq.*

the distinction between our national and municipal politics? In the former sphere the citizens study, know, and act upon political questions. In the cities they do neither; and public interests are placed in the hands of professional politicians who act often from base and sordid motives. Common citizenship will tend to elevate and enlighten all the citizens, and the healthful influences resulting therefrom will gradually permeate into the manners, morals, and legislation of all the countries involved.

III.—TO ESTABLISH FREEDOM OF COMMERCIAL INTERCOURSE AND RELATIONS BETWEEN THE COUNTRIES INVOLVED, TO THE SAME EXTENT AS THAT WHICH EXISTS BETWEEN THE DIFFERENT STATES CONSTITUTING THE UNITED STATES OF AMERICA

It would be quite useless to create common citizenship, it would be a vain endeavour to form a lasting union between the English-speaking people, unless free and unrestricted commercial relations were established between them. Every port which they own or control must always be wide open to the citizens of each nation. The same liberal commercial relations must be permitted between the United States and the British Empire as now exist under the Constitution between the citizens of different States of the Union.

Montesquieu says that commerce is a cure for the most destructive prejudices, and that peace is the natural result of trade.

We can behold its successful and beneficent effect upon the States of our American Union. We witness the disastrous influence of restricted trade relations between Canada and the United States.

These two examples cover the whole field of discussion and render elaboration useless. Each American State has grown and thrived under the principle of free commerce. It regulates production and sale, and confines the inhabitants of each section to the cultivation or manufacture of those articles which surrounding conditions justify; it limits and attaches them to that industry which is most congenial and profitable. To the restless, discontented, unlucky, or unfortunate classes—of which there are always plenty—there is the chance to go elsewhere, a door always open through which they can pass into another State under the same citizenship, where different pursuits are followed more in keeping with their tastes and knowledge. A floating population, drifting from one place to another with perfect freedom and security, will finally settle in some locality where they can make use of whatever knowledge they possess, with a direct benefit to themselves and the place where they ultimately settle.

Lord Bacon saw the importance of commercial freedom in welding the bonds between England and Scotland, using the argument with skill and force in his advocacy for union between them:

"Thirdly, for so much as the principal degree to union is communion and participation of mutual commodities and benefits, it appeared to us to follow next in order that the commerce between both nations be set open and free, so as the commodities and provisions of either may pass and flow to and fro without any stops or obstructions into the veins of the whole body, for the better sustentation and comfort of all the parts, with caution, nevertheless, that the vital nourishment be not so drawn into one part as it may endanger a consumption and withering of the other."[77]

And it was in the spirit of this advice that the union was, long afterwards, formed. It was the offer of free trade tendered by the Godolphin administration which finally overcame the national prejudices of the Scottish people. The results, after a brief period of adjustment to new conditions, amply justified the wisdom of the forecast: it is not necessary that I should again state them. To those who recall the former relations of the two countries as they had existed for centuries, they will appear among the most marvellous recorded in history.

It will not be necessary here to cite authorities. I am not dealing with an open question. The value of commerce, which, unless it is free, ceases to be commerce, in regulating the intercourse between nations, in promoting peace, in carrying forward the work of civilisation, has been recognised by every thinker and every philanthropist in every age since the world emerged from pure barbarism.

It was the full realisation of this truth and necessity that drove the thirteen original States into forming a federative union, quite as much as political reasons. The same causes operated upon the Canadians in their federative union, and they must be predominant features in the formation of the political ligament which binds the English-speaking peoples in a perpetual league.

There are two unmistakable and substantial benefits which result from commercial reciprocity: first, joint business interests represented by men of both countries have a direct tendency to mutual understandings in the individuals; second, in the governments, as giving them objects of common protection and support.

How quickly these benefits will be realised in the union of the English-speaking peoples must be most obvious to all of us in the light of our present and past history.

IV.—GREAT BRITAIN AND THE UNITED STATES (I) TO COIN GOLD, SILVER, NICKEL AND COPPER MONEY, NOT DISPLAYING THE SAME DEVICES OR MOTTOES, BUT POSSESSING AN EQUAL MONEY VALUE, AND INTERCHANGEABLE EVERYWHERE WITHIN THE LIMITS COVERED BY THE TREATY, AND (2) TO ESTABLISH A UNIFORM STANDARD OF WEIGHTS AND MEASURES

I. The Same Gold, Silver, Nickel And Copper Money

The influence of a uniform standard of money upon a people in uniting them

[77] Certificate prepared by Lord Bacon upon the proposed union of England and Scotland.—Lord Bacon's *Works,* vol. v., p. 43.

is most obvious. In fact, I know of no stronger element to educate a people in political and commercial sympathy than the use of interchangeable coins, possessing an equal money value, and circulating freely among them—money, bearing the same name for each denomination, with different national designs on the obverse side, but perhaps similar characters and figures could be used on the reverse side.

The adoption of coins of the same value among all the Anglo-Saxon peoples would be perhaps next in importance to language and literature in binding them firmly together.

An element conspicuously noticed in the nationalisation or unification of different nations or tribes is a common money-system. Mommsen[78] in speaking of the unification of Italy by Rome, says:

"Lastly, Rome, as head of the Romano-Italian confederacy, not only entered into the Hellenistic state-system, but also conformed to the Hellenic system of moneys and coins. Up to this time the different communities of northern and central Italy, with few exceptions, had struck only a copper currency; the south Italian towns again universally had a currency of silver, and there were as many legal standards and systems of coinage as there were sovereign communities in Italy. In 485 all these local mints were restricted to the issuing of small coin; a general standard of currency applicable to all Italy was introduced and the coining of the currency was centralised in Rome; Capua alone continued to retain its own silver coinage struck in the name of Rome, but after a different standard."

I do not make any definite suggestion as to the size, design, or names of the different species of coins. This is not the place for such details.

Canada has already made an important step in this direction. She has freely followed the United States of America in her silver coins, which, with the exception of the inscriptions, are practically the same as those issued by our own Government—she has her half-dollars, twenty-five-, ten-, and five-cent pieces.[79]

II.—*To Establish A Uniform Standard Of Weights And Measures*

Quite apart from the plan heretofore outlined, it is highly important as an element of mutual commercial benefit that the English-speaking people should establish among themselves a uniform standard of weights and measures. It would facilitate and make easy commercial freedom, and guarantee to our race that an *entente*, if established, would be built upon sound foundations. It would likewise impress upon foreign nations the strength of our compact. Once we have adopted a common monetary system, supplemented it with a uniform standard of weights and measures, and carried into effect the other suggestions heretofore advocated, the union of the English-speaking people is a *fait accompli*. Thus the two richest and most powerful nations of the world would be knit together by all the elements of sentiment and selfishness, and their moral force and influence would be predominating.

---

[78] Vol. ii., p. 87.

[79] See also in this connection extracts from *A History of Currency in the British Colonies*, by Robert Chalmers, B.A., of Oriel College and of her Majesty's Treasury.

V.—IN CASE OF ANY DISPUTE HEREAFTER OCCURRING BETWEEN GREAT BRITAIN, OR ANY OF HER COLONIES, AND THE UNITED STATES, THE SAME TO BE REFERRED TO A SUPREME COURT OF ARBITRATION TO BE CREATED AND ORGANISED UPON SUBSTANTIALLY THE FOLLOWING LINES:

(*a*) All disputes between the signatories to be referred to, and settled by, this tribunal.

(*b*) The court to be composed of twelve arbitrators, as follows: Six to be selected by England and the same number by the United States.

The King of England to appoint the Chancellor of England, a member of the House of Lords, a member of the House of Commons, a banker, a merchant, and the president or chairman of the leading industrial or labour organisation of the empire. The President of the United States to choose a judge of the Supreme Court of the United States, a member of the United States Senate, a member of the House of Representatives, a banker, a merchant, and the president or chairman of the leading industrial or labour organisation of the United States.

(*c*) The first meeting of the arbitrators to be held, say, within ninety days after their appointment.

(*d*) At their first meeting, without regard to whether any quarrel or dispute has arisen to be submitted to them, to select an umpire, who shall cast the final vote in case of a tie.

By selecting an umpire in the beginning, the Arbitration Court is fully organised and always ready to act. After a dispute has arisen the choice of an umpire becomes most delicate and difficult and sometimes insuperable.

CONCLUSION

THE STATE OF PUBLIC OPINION UPON THE QUESTION OF ANGLO-SAXON ALLIANCE

BEFORE the Spanish-American War a discussion of the subjects embraced in this book would have been premature. Professor Dicey, appealing through a magazine article, in April, 1897 (hereafter quoted), for a "common citizenship" for all Englishmen and Americans, was compelled to acknowledge a year later that his proposal "fell flat," and that for his disinterested efforts he received a few friendly but discouraging letters!

The times have changed, and the buds of great political and international questions, which have hung so long upon the trees of history, green and immature, have suddenly ripened.

The Spanish War peeped "through the blanket of the dark" and luminously lit up the American nation to the gaze of an astonished world. The problem which agitates the powers and the press of continental Europe is the future of the so-called "Anglo-Saxon" race, and the necessity and possibility of combining the nations of the world against it.

The immature subject of an English-American alliance, which a few years ago could not awaken the interest of the people of the two nations, and was looked upon as an impracticable theory of visionary men, is now become momentous by reason of grim facts.

The courage and boldness which a writer must possess to open to public gaze new and untrodden fields of thought are no longer indispensable qualities to the present task. All that is now required is a substantial and satisfactory method of accomplishing the desired end.

It is interesting, if not essential, to explore the state of public opinion upon this subject. How far has public thought progressed in this direction? What view is entertained of it by the four great organs of public opinion of the two nations: the Press, the Pulpit, the Bar, the Stage?

Notwithstanding a somewhat diligent search for all literature bearing upon the subject, I have doubtless overlooked many, perhaps some of the best, contributions. From most of those I have seen, I will now give extracts. The newspaper articles it is impossible to quote from—they are too numerous. Besides, quotations from them in most cases would be unjust and unsatisfactory.

The Press of England and the United States has only treated this great question in a desultory and superficial way, because there has been no definite question before the two nations for discussion. So far as I can judge, however, a fair majority of the newspapers favour the general suggestion of a "closer bond of sympathy," a "better understanding," and an utter renunciation of an appeal to arms to settle disputes between the United States and Great Britain. How these things will be accomplished they do not consider, except that a majority of the newspapers favour the adoption of an arbitration treaty.

The Bar, yet representing, shall I say, the serious, sober, best thought of the two nations, takes no combined action upon public questions. Its organisation, so far as matters are involved which do not directly affect its members or its *esprit du corps*, is merely formal. Its views can be gathered from individual sources only, and from articles which individual members contribute to the literature of the day. Those I have found and quote from, favour an alliance.

The Pulpit has been outspoken and enthusiastic from the commencement in its advocacy of an alliance.

The Stage, always ready to catch the sentiments of the hour, has, with its usual aptness and scenic skill, entwined England and the United States together in friendly embrace; and grotesque and exaggerated allusions to a coalition "to whip all the world," have been liberally and vociferously applauded.

I now give the quotations promiscuously. The italics are my own. They are made to show the very gist of the author's opinion.

The first article that came under my notice is, strangely enough, the most definite in its purpose and conclusion, and was published in April, 1897, by Professor Dicey, under the title of "A Common Citizenship for the English Races."[80]

Professor Dicey states that his "aim is to establish the possibility and advocate the policy of instituting a common citizenship for all Englishmen and Americans." He says:

"My proposal is summarily this: That England and the United States should, by concurrent and appropriate legislation, create such a common citizenship, or, to put the matter in a more concrete and therefore in a more intelligible form, that an act of the Imperial Parliament should make every citizen of the United States, during the continuance of peace between England and America, a British subject, and that simultaneously an act of Congress should make every British subject, during the continuance of such peace, a citizen of the United States. . . .

"Common citizenship, or isopolity, has no necessary connection whatever with national or political unity. My proposal is not designed to limit the complete national independence either of England or of the United States. *It would be not only an absurdity, but almost an act of lunacy, to devise or defend a scheme for turning England and America into one state.* It is as impossible, as, were it possible, it would be undesirable, that Washington should be ruled by a government in London, or that London should be ruled by a government in Washington.

---

[80] *Contemporary Review*, April, 1897.

". . . What my proposal does aim at is, in short, not political unity, but, in strictness, common citizenship. Were it carried into effect, the net result would be that every American citizen would, on landing at Liverpool, possess the same civil and political rights as would, say, an inhabitant of Victoria who landed at the same moment from the same boat; and that an Englishman who stepped for the first time on American soil would possess there all the civil and political rights which would necessarily belong to an American citizen who, having been born abroad, had for the first time entered the United States."

Mr. James Bryce, in an article favouring any proper means to establish an alliance between the two countries, says[81]:

"Meantime there are things which may be done at once to cement and perpetuate the good relations which happily prevail. One is the conclusion of a general arbitration treaty providing for the amicable settlement of all differences which may hereafter arise between the nations. Another is the agreement to render services to each other; such, for instance, as giving to a citizen of either nation the right to invoke the good offices of the diplomatic or consular representatives of the other in a place where his own government has no representative; or [following the proposition of Professor Dicey, heretofore referred to] *such as the recognition of a common citizenship, securing to the citizens of each in the country of the other, certain rights not enjoyed by other foreigners."*

Mr. Joseph Chamberlain, England's Secretary for the Colonies,[82] states his views upon the subject as follows:

"So far as the United Kingdom is concerned, it may be taken as a fact that the British nation would welcome any approach to this conclusion, *that there is hardly any length to which they would not go in response to American advances,* and that they would not shrink even from an alliance *contra mundum,* if the need should ever arise, in defence of the ideals of the Anglo-Saxon race — of humanity, justice, freedom, and equality of opportunity.

"It must not be supposed, however, that in accepting an alliance as a possible and welcome contingency, *anything in the nature of a permanent or general alliance is either desirable or practicable.*

"Any attempt to pledge the two nations beforehand to combine defensive and offensive action in all circumstances must inevitably break down and be a source of danger instead of strength. All therefore that the most sanguine advocate of an alliance can contemplate is *that the United States and Great Britain should keep in close touch with each other, and that whenever their policy and their interests are identical they should be prepared to concert together the necessary measures for their defence.*

"It is to such a course of action that Washington seems to point when he says: 'Taking care always to keep ourselves, by suitable establishments, in a respectable defensive posture, we may safely trust to temporary alliances for extraordinary emergencies.'"

---

[81] *Atlantic Monthly,* July, 1898.
[82] *Scribner's Magazine,* December, 1898.

Walter Charles Copeland, favouring the proposed Anglo-American Alliance, says:

"Nor ought we to remain satisfied with the moral alliance which is, and always will be, and probably always would have been, formed at a Pinch between the branches of the Anglo-Saxon race. True, it may be considered by our statesmen in their wisdom that the common interest will be served best by a secret alliance, or a more subtle understanding. Anyway, there is ample scope for the work of a league or association, or for more than one, devoted to the great purpose of correcting misapprehensions and moulding public opinion on both sides."[83]

Sir Charles Dilke sympathises with the movement, but believes there is no chance of a permanent alliance with the United States as matters now stand:

"I have seen," he says, "no inclination expressed across the Atlantic by the responsible leaders of political opinion pointing towards the conclusion of any instrument consecrating so startling a departure from the American policy of the past."[84]

The same author concludes an article[85] entitled "The Future Relations of Great Britain and the United States" as follows:

"The issue which lies behind this interesting, but perplexing, study of the future relations of our countries is no less than the decision whether in the second half of the next century the dominant interest in the world is to be Anglo-American or Russian. When I say Anglo-American, I in no way forget the position in the southern hemisphere of our own great colonies; but I include them under the first half of my compound name, Germans may be inclined to take offence at the above hint of prophecy. It is certain that for a long time to come the Prussian army must be an enormous factor in the Continental politics of the Old World. On the other hand, considered as a World-Power, Germany can hardly rank, even in the time of our remote descendants, on a level with the Russian Empire, or with the Anglo-Saxon combination, should the latter come into existence and survive.

"The matter which I have discussed in this article is no new one for me. Writing on Europe in 1886-87, I said, referring to what I had written in 1866-67:

"In 'Greater Britain' the doctrine which I attempted to lay down was that ... the English-speaking ... lands should attract a larger share of the attention of the inhabitants of the United Kingdom; that in all these, whether subject or not subject to the British rule, the English race was essentially the same in its most marked characteristics; that in the principal English-speaking country not subject to the Queen—the United States—England had imposed her tongue and laws upon the offshoots of Germany, Scandinavia, Spain, and I might now add, Russia; and that the dominance of our language throughout this powerful and enormous country ... must produce in the future political phenomena to which our attention ought more persistently to be called.

---

[83] *Westminster Review*, August, 1898.
[84] *Pall Mall Magazine*, September, 1898.
[85] *Forum*, January, 1899.

"The prophecy has come true. *It is for the Americans of the United States to decide how far toward firm alliance what I called 'the tie of blood and tongue and history and letters' shall be carried.*"

Mr. A. W. Tourgee, in an article entitled "The Twentieth Century Peacemakers,"[86] discussed with great power the subject involved here. *Inter alia* he says:

"So well known and universally acknowledged is this characteristic of the Anglo-Saxon family, that one wonders how so much stress should have been laid on community of origin and identity of civilisation by the advocates of a better understanding between its two branches, and so little attention given to the one thing needful to efficient co-operation between political organisms — to wit, *a common aim and purpose.* Especially is this notable when we reflect that conditions not difficult to define clearly demonstrate that some closer relation between Great Britain and the United States *is not only a desirable possibility, but an inevitable and quick-coming necessity.* Instead of requiring advocacy at the hands of any party or individuals, the public sentiment of two great nations has outrun the sagacity of leaders, and with that curious instinct which often controls what seems to be a blind emotion, has truly forecast world-conditions, that must, in a very brief time, compel the two countries to strike hands for the preservation of the peace of the world, and the maintenance of those ideals which the Anglo-Saxon holds above any consideration of material or political advantage. For despite his enterprise and greed, the Anglo-Saxon, more willingly than any other stock, lends ear to Ruskin's 'strange people who have other loves than those of wealth, and other interests than those of commerce.' . . .

"The Anglo-Saxon alone offers to the semi-civilised peoples that come under his control the advantages of intellectual and material development. The schoolhouse, the free press, agricultural and commercial development, are inseparable incidents of Anglo-Saxon sway. Political and material betterment are the prizes it offers to the laggards in civilisation who come beneath its rule. This is what England offers in India, Egypt, and the Soudan; what the United States offers in the West Indies and the Philippines."

In speaking of the possibility of a combination of other powers against the Anglo-Saxon race, the same author says:

"Eliminate the United States from the problem, guarantee her neutrality, and there is little doubt that before the dawn of the twentieth century the civilised world would be arrayed in arms against Great Britain."

"Whether they desire it or not, the necessities of the world's life, the preservation of their own political ideals, and the commercial and economic conditions which they confront must soon compel a *closer entente* between these two great peoples. They are the peacemakers of the twentieth century, the protectors of the world's liberty, of free economic development, and of the weak nationalities of the earth. With nations as with men, peace is usually the result of apprehension of consequences that might ensue from conflict. A free people, a government based on public opinion, a people whose interests demand commercial opportunity, is

[86] *Contemporary Review,* June, 1899.

always in favour of peace. They may be stirred to war by injustice or oppression or in assertion of the rights and liberties of others, but are rarely moved to a war of aggression or for mere national aggrandisement. Commercial character is the surest guarantee of peaceful purpose, and the closer union of the two greatest commercial nations of the world is the strongest possible security for the world's peace."

Sir Richard Temple, in an article[87] entitled "An Anglo-American *vs.* a European Combination," makes an interesting analysis of the physical and material elements which would enter into such a struggle. He concludes as follows:

"To us who believe in the superior power of the two English-speaking nations in comparison with other races taken together, the question may be put whether such a condition is morally and intellectually beneficial to us. I am not concerned, however, here to attempt any answer to such a question, which is wholly a matter of opinion. This article relates not at all to opinion, but only to facts.

"I will conclude the Anglo-American case with a metaphor. Britain is like a Grand Old Dame, well preserved and still maintaining the vigour and activity of her youth. Her eye is not dimmed by age; her strong hand is not weakened by the lapse of centuries. She has been the mother of many children, and has sometimes had troubles in her family. But in recent times she has been on good terms with all her offspring, all over the world. She would not suffer them to be beaten in the race of nations. If any of them were to fall into danger, she would bring out her stores, collected through many generations, in their support. If, on the other hand, she were to be hard pressed by any hostile combination, then her stalwart sons would gather round her."

Hon. David Mills, Canadian Minister of Justice,[88] under the title of "Which Shall Dominate—Saxon or Slav?", makes a very intelligent analysis of the question of the relative position of the Anglo-Saxon race against the continental powers of Europe. He says:

"In the highest sense the United States has not, and cannot have, an independent existence. Her fortune is inseparably associated with the race to which she belongs, in which her future is wrapt up, and in which she lives and moves and has her being. The unity between the United States and the British Empire is a matter both of race and growth. They touch each other, and as peoples unite and great states rise, they must be, for all great international purposes, one people. They are parts of the same race, whose extension is being pushed more and more rapidly forward by the sleepless energy of individual men, under the protection of the United Kingdom, into barbarous regions where they are acquiring new standing-room for the formation of new states. In science, in literature, in government, in religion, in industrial pursuits, and in the conception of human rights and of human duties, they are one people, having common aims, a common origin, and from their necessary relations a common destiny. . . .

"*The interests of the world call for Anglo-Saxon alliance.* Let not the British Empire

[87] *North American Review,* September, 1898.
[88] *North American Review,* June, 1898.

and the United States revive, after the lapse of centuries, the old contest of Judah and Ephraim; but, remembering that their interests are one, as the race is one, *let them stand together*, to maintain the ascendency which they will hold as long as Providence fits them to lead; which will be as long as, in their dealings with those beneath them, they are actuated by principles of justice and truth."

Rear-Admiral Lord Charles Beresford, in an article entitled "An Anglo-American Alliance,"[89] exclaims:

"Much has been said for an Anglo-American alliance. Perhaps 'alliance' is not the right word. We are already of the same blood, the same feeling, the same religion, and the same language. Now all that is necessary is to know each other better. England and America could form the most powerful alliance possible, because they are the two most patriotic countries in the world; because they alone, of all the nations, have an army and navy without conscription. . . . With the United States and England combined, we could well afford to smile at our enemies."

An article which deserves to be carefully read is that by Prof. George Burton Adams[90] entitled "A Century of Anglo-Saxon Expansion."

"The simple truth is," says this writer, "that, great as have been the demands upon the race to create the history of the past in which we rejoice, the demands of the future will be even greater. It is the result of this history, the proper and fitting result, that we are now brought to the supreme test of racial ability. The nineteenth century, truly considered, is but an age of preliminary and introductory expansion. If the genius of the race fail not; if calm submission to the law, unwavering devotion to the task in hand, steady refusal to follow glittering allurements or hasty choices, may still be our leading traits; if we may trust our sons to equal our fathers' deeds of self-devotion without the hope of fame, then is the achievement of the nineteenth century but a preparing of the way for the vaster expansion of the twentieth, — for the founding, not of the empire of the race, but of the united commonwealth of all nations.

"But if these things fail us, if this so rapid growth has exhausted the moral stamina of the race, if by its unsettling hurry it has destroyed our power of patient self-control, then shall we repeat the history of other empires. This great fabric of ours, which, as far as human judgment can discern, *needs but closer union to be secure against the shock of every danger from without*, will in that case break asunder and fall, from its own inner decay. History will then record that the nineteenth century was our greatest but our final era of expansion."

Mr. Carl Schurz[91] ends an article upon the subject as follows:

"As to the manner in which the friendly feeling now existing can be given a tangible expression, Mr. Bryce has made some valuable suggestions. The first thing to be accomplished is the conclusion of an arbitration treaty covering all kinds of differences, and thus recognising that no quarrels can possibly arise be-

[89] *The Independent*, February 23, 1899.
[90] *Atlantic Monthly*, April, 1897.
[91] *Ibid.*, October, 1898.

tween the two nations which would not be capable of amicable composition, and that under no circumstances will any less pacific method of settlement be desired on either side. In fact, the amendments disfiguring beyond recognition the arbitration treaty which two years ago was before the Senate, and its final defeat, were the last effective stroke of the old anti-British jingoism, for which amends should now be made by a prompt resumption of negotiations for the accomplishment of that great object. In this way the Anglo-American friendship will signalise itself to the world by an act that will not only benefit the two countries immediately concerned, but set an example to other nations which, if generally followed, will do more for the peace and happiness of mankind and the progress of civilisation than anything that can be effected by armies and navies."

"The Proposed Anglo-American Alliance" is strongly advocated by Charles A. Gardiner, Esq., of the New York Bar, in a forcibly written pamphlet[92] in which he says:

"An alliance between England and America to adjust their controversies by means of enlightened arbitration has already been introduced into practical politics. The time is opportune for its re-introduction. If the friendly sentiments at Westminster and Washington should be promptly utilised to enact a treaty of arbitration, such an alliance would be justified on every ground of common and reciprocal interests, would have the moral and political support of both nations, would establish a most beneficent precedent for the international adjustment of the affairs of mankind, and would do more than any other single act to make possible the disarmament of nations and the maintenance of universal peace. . . .

"The grandest thought of the century is this convergence of the Anglo-Saxon race. What more ennobling conception can engage the attention of any association of scholars and thinkers? As citizens and individuals our duties ally us with this beneficent movement. Let us promote a unity already begun; let us encourage the common interests and sentiments of the nations; let us, so far as in us lies, consummate in our day that alliance of kin predicted by the wise and good of three generations, as the 'noblest, most beneficial, most peaceful primacy ever presented to the heart and understanding of man.'"

In an article called "The English-speaking Brotherhood," Professor Charles Waldstein,[93] after summarising the elements that exist in common between the two countries, says:

"Now, when any group of people have all these eight elements in common, *they ought of necessity to form a political unity;* and when a group of people have not the first of these factors [the same country], but are essentially kin in the remaining seven, they ought to develop some close form of lasting amity. In the case of the people of Great Britain and of the United States, seven of these leading features are actively present.

"It may even be held that the first condition, a common country, which would make of the two peoples one nation, in some sense exists for them. At all events, a

[92] *Questions of the Day*, No. XCII., p. 27. published by G. P. Putnam's Sons.
[93] *North American Review*, August, 1898.

country is sufficiently common to them to supply sentimental unity in this direction. . . .

"Leaving the question of a common country, the bond of union becomes closer the further we proceed with the other essential influences which make for unity, when once we drop the misleading and wholly illusory ethnological basis of nationality, and take into account the process of real history. We then must acknowledge that the people of Great Britain and of the United States are of one nationality."

"The Basis of an Anglo-American Understanding," by the Rev. Lyman Abbott,[94] concludes as follows:

"Thus far I have suggested only 'a good understanding,' because this is immediately practicable, yet I have in my imagination an ideal toward which such a good understanding might tend, but which would far transcend anything suggested by that somewhat vague phrase. Let us suppose, then, that Great Britain and the United States were to enter into *an alliance* involving these three elements: first, *absolute reciprocity of trade; second, a tribunal to which should be referred for settlement, as a matter of course, all questions arising between the two nations,* as now all questions arising between the various states of this Union are referred to the Supreme Court of the United States; *third, a mutual pledge that an assault on one should be regarded as an assault on both, so that as towards other nations these two would be united as the various states of this Union stand united towards all other states. Such an alliance would include not only our own country and the British Isles, but all the colonies and dependencies of Great Britain — Canada,* Australasia, and in time such provinces in Asia and Africa as are under British domination and administration. It would unite in the furtherance of a Christian civilisation all the Anglo-Saxon peoples, and all the peoples acting under the guidance and controlling influence of Anglo-Saxon leaders, it would gradually draw into itself all other peoples of like minds, though of foreign race, such as, in the far east, the people of Japan. It would create *a new confederation* based on principles and ideas not on tradition, and bounded by the possibilities of human development not by geographical lines. It would give a new significance to the motto *E Pluribus Unum,* and would create a new United States of the World of which the United States of America would be a component part."

Mr. Julian Ralph ends an article,[95] in which he closely examines the causes of the present prejudice existing between the two countries, with this sentence:

"As a last word upon the subject of the *mooted alliance,* my own belief is that it *is not as practicable or as advisable as the good understanding* that seems to have already been brought about without too suspicious a show of anxiety on either side, without elaborate discussion, and without formal agreement, I agree with the wisest American to whom I have spoken on the subject, and who said a year ago, when there was no such roseate outlook as this of to-day, 'It may be delayed, and we may even quarrel with England before it is brought about, but, nevertheless, the certain destiny of the two peoples *is to stand together for the maintenance of order,*

____

[94] *North American Review,* May, 1898.
[95] *Harper's New Monthly Magazine,* February, 1899.

justice, and humanity, and for the extension of a higher form of civilisation than any other nations stand for."

Mr. James K. Hosmer, in an article entitled "The American Evolution: Dependence, Independence, Interdependence,"[96] after presenting a number of contemporaneous English authorities,"1 to show that the American Revolution was inevitable, and in the true interests of the English people themselves, and after quoting a letter which John Bright wrote in 1887 to the Committee for the Celebration of the Centennial of the American Constitution, wherein he states—" As you advance in the second century of your national life, may we not ask *that our two nations may become one people?"* closes as follows:

"The townships make up the county, the counties the state, the states the United States. What is to hinder a further extension of the federal principle, *so that finally we may have a vaster United States, whose members shall be, as empire State, America; then the mother, England; and lastly the great English dependencies, so populous and thoroughly developed that they may justly stand co-ordinate?* It cannot be said that this is an unreasonable or Utopian anticipation. Dependence was right in its day; but for English help colonial America would have become a province of France. Independence was and is right. It was well for us, and for Britain too, that we were split apart. Washington, as the main agent in the separation, is justly the most venerated name in our history. But _inter_dependence, too, will in its day be right; and great indeed will be that statesman of the future who shall reconstitute the family bond, conciliate the members into an equal brotherhood, found the vaster union which must be the next great step towards the universal fraternity of man, when patriotism may be merged into a love that will take in all humanity.

"Such suggestions as have just been made are sure to be opposed both in England and America. We on our side cite England's oppression of Ireland, the rapacity with which in all parts of the world she has often enlarged her boundaries, the brutality with which she has trampled upon the rights of weaker men. They cite against America her 'century of dishonour' in the treatment of the Indians, the corruption of her cities, the ruffian's knife and pistol, ready to murder on slight provocation, the prevalence of lynch law over all other law in great districts, her yellow journalism. Indeed, it is a sad tale of shortcoming for both countries. Yet in the case of each the evil is balanced by a thousand things great and good, and the welfare of the world depends upon the growth and prosperity of the English-speaking lands as upon nothing else. The welfare of the world depends upon their accord; and no other circumstance at the present moment is so fraught with hope as that, in the midst of the heavy embarrassments that beset both England and America, the long-sundered kindred slowly gravitate toward alliance."[97]

Mr. B. O. Flower contributes an article to the discussion,[98] entitled "The Proposed Federation of the Anglo-Saxon Nations," favouring an alliance. The key-

---

[96] *Atlantic Monthly,* July, 1898.
[97] See, also, by the same author, *A Short History of Anglo-Saxon Freedom,* 1890.
[98] *Arena,* August, 1898.

note of his views is contained in this passage[99]:

"But beyond a common blood, language, and mutual interests, rises the factor which above all others is fundamental, and which more than aught else makes such an alliance worthy of serious consideration, and that *is the common ideal or goal to which all the moral energies of both people are moving, the spirit which permeates all English-speaking nations, namely, popular sovereignty, or self-government; that is, republicanism in essence.*"[100]

Mr. Richard Olney, in a convincing argument[101] on international isolation of the United States, explains the doctrine of Washington's warning to his countrymen, "It is our true policy to steer clear of permanent alliances with any portion of the foreign world," as follows:

"The Washington rule of isolation, then, proves on examination to have a much narrower scope than the generally accepted versions given to it. Those versions of it may and undoubtedly do find countenance in loose and general and unconsidered statements of public men both of the Washington era and of later times, . . . Nothing can be more obvious, therefore, than that the conditions for which Washington made his rule no longer exist. . . . There is a patriotism of race as well as of country—and the Anglo-American is as little likely to be indifferent to the one as to the other. Family quarrels there have been heretofore and doubtless there will be again, and the two peoples, at a safe distance which the broad Atlantic interposes, take with each other liberties of speech which only the fondest and dearest relatives indulge in. Nevertheless, they would be found standing together against any alien foe by whom either was menaced with destruction or irreparable calamity, it is not permissible to doubt. Nothing less could be expected of the close community between them in origin, speech, thought, literature, institutions, ideals—in the kind and degree of the civilisation enjoyed by both."

In an article entitled "Shall the United States be Europeanised?"[102] Mr. John Clark Ridpath violently opposes an alliance. He states:

"The time has come when the United States must gravitate rapidly *towards* Europe or else diverge *from* Europe as far and as fast as possible.

"This is an overwhelming alternative which forces itself upon the American people at the close of the nineteenth century; in the twentieth we shall be either Europeanised or democratized—the one or the other. There is no place of stable equilibrium between the two. This is true for the reason that there can be no such thing as a democratic monarchy; no such thing as a monarchical republic; no such thing as a popular aristocracy; no such thing as a democracy of nabobs.

"The twentieth century will bring us either to democracy unequivocal or to empire absolute. All hybrid combinations of the two are unstable; they break and

[99] Pp. 225, 226.
[100] See, also, "The Anglo-American Future," by Frederick Greenwood, *The Nineteenth Century,* July, 1898.
[101] *Atlantic Monthly,* May, 1898.
[102] *Arena,* December, 1897.

pass away. Either the one type or the other must be established in our Western hemisphere. The democratic Republic which we *thought* we had, and which we so greatly prized and fought for, must now sheer off *from* Europe altogether, or else sail quietly back *to* Europe and come to anchor. Shall we or shall we not go thither?"

In another article, entitled "The United States and the Concert of Europe,"[103] he says:

"In the first place, I inquire, what is the *meaning* of the proposed alliance between the United States and Great Britain? What *kind* of an alliance is it that we are asked to enter? Is it an alliance of mere sympathies between the people of the United States and the people of the British Isles? Or is it a league which contemplates a union of military resources, defensive and offensive, one or both? Is it a temporary joining of forces for specific purposes in relation to the existing Spanish War? Is it a coalescence of British and American institutions? Is it a civil and political union which is contemplated? Is it a government alliance in the sense that the government of Great Britain and the government of the United States shall be and act as one? And if so, *which one* shall it be? Under which flag is the alliance to be made? Are we, when the union shall be effected, to follow the standard of St. George, or are we to march under the star-banner of our fathers? Whose flag is to prevail? Whose institutional structure is to be accepted for both nations? Of a certainty, we cannot march under both flags. It must be under the one or the other. Which shall it be? Shall we take the flag of the British Empire, or the flag of American Democracy?"

Mr. R.E. Kingsford, in an article entitled "Roma! Cave Tibi!"[104] which he commences with a fervent declaration of love for England and Englishmen, continues:

"Do you care to be warned, or do you wish to continue in a course which will split up your Empire? It is time to speak plainly and it is time for us to understand one another. No matter how much we admire you, no matter how much we reverence you, no matter how much we are ready to submit to neglect at your hands, the time has come when the future course of our relations must be settled. We feel very sore at your preference for the United States. We have been brought up to think that you are right and that they are wrong. We believe in your system of government as opposed to theirs. Both cannot be right. We have always thought that the people ruled in England, while the mob ruled in the United States. But, alas! We are beginning to think that we have been wrong. We see you Englishmen caressing the Americans, flattering them, submitting to them, backing out of declarations made as to what you were going to do until they stepped in and told you to stop. We see our public men, almost without exception, in every speech they make, allude fondly in round set terms to their 'kin beyond the seas.' Will nothing open your eyes? Will you not see that these people are not your kin? They are aliens. Will you not understand that they do not care two straws about you? Their idea is that they are the mightiest nation upon earth. They consider that they own

---

[103] *Arena*, August, 1898.
[104] *Canadian Magazine*, January, 1899

the Continent of North America and that your presence on that continent is an anachronism and an absurdity. Surely they have told you so plainly enough. Do you think that by protesting so much admiration for them you will disarm them? If you do, you are making a huge mistake which you will bitterly pay for. . . .

"I warn you, Englishmen, you are treading on dangerous ground. The British Lion is hugging and slobbering over the American Eagle. But that scrawny bird is only submitting to be embraced. The situation is an illustration of the French Proverb, that there is always one who loves (England), and one who is loved (the United States.) Presently the Eagle's beak will tear the Lion's flesh, and the Eagle's talons tear the Lion's side. Then there will be a roar of astonished anger. But the mistake will have been made, the mischief will have been done. Cease this Anglo-American nonsense. Rely on your own colonies. Establish inter-Imperial tariffs. . . .

"If you persist in allowing yourselves to be cozened by your belief or trust in American good-will, so that you neglect or slight your loyal and true Canadian fellow-subjects, you will lose Canada, you will lose your West India Islands, and then how long will the rest of your Empire last? Roma! Cave Tibi!"

In an editorial from the *Canadian Magazine* for August, 1898, entitled "A Hasty Alliance," the learned editor writes as follows:

"During the past two months the proposed Anglo-American Understanding has occupied a great deal of attention in Great Britain and Canada, and a very fair amount of similar enthusiasm in the United States. The idea of an understanding which will enable both branches of the English race—if it may be called such—to work side by side, with one aim and one mission, is certainly most worthy. If it can be successfully carried into performance, it will be the most important political development of the nineteenth century.

"The officials of Great Britain have always been courteous, and kind, and considerate to the United States. These gentlemen have gone so far as to pay the United States a million dollars more for Alabama claims than was actually necessary. They gave up half the State of Maine because they did not care to remark that a certain map was a forgery. They have always used respectable language about or to the United States. When, therefore, they now say that they value United States friendship and approve of Anglo-Saxon unity, I cannot accuse them of inconsistency. Nor can I in my own mind feel that they are insincere. . . .

"Personally, I have no objection to Lord Wolseley, Lord Dufferin, Sir Wilfred Laurier, and Sir Charles Tupper expressing their appreciation of the United States, and their desire to see permanent friendly relations between the two countries. These gentlemen represent the officialdom of Great Britain and of Canada, and are speaking semi-officially. They are, without doubt, quite sincere in their desire to have the two branches of the nation act in unison. But I do object to their pushing Mr. Chamberlain's idea with too much cheap publicity. Let them say what they think and feel without descending to fulsome flattery which they may some day wish they had left unsaid."

In "Commercial Relations between Canada and the United States," by Robert

McConnell, editor of the *Halifax Morning Herald*,[105] the writer states:

"We believe further that the time has gone by when American politicians can woo Canada into a political union even by a policy of friendliness and close commercial relations. Without in any way seeking to disparage the United States as a great nation, and her people as worthy of the Anglo-Saxon stock from which they sprang, the Canadian people feel that theirs is a higher national and political destiny—to be one of the great family of Anglo-Saxon nations comprising a worldwide British Empire, whose mission is to civilise, enlighten, and christianise the people who come under her sway, and by the genius of free institutions and the influence of a world-wide, peace-producing, and humanising commerce to raise strong barriers against the demon of war and promote peace and good-will among the nations. Why should not the United States come into the Anglo-Saxon family of nations, and have a share in such noble work? There is room enough and scope enough on this continent for the two Anglo-Saxon nations—Canada and the United States—daughters of a common mother, custodians of a common liberty—to work out their separate destinies without being jealous of each other or coveting each other's patrimony and birthright. They can maintain a friendly and honourable rivalry in the world of industry and commerce, and at the same time co-operate heartily in promoting the arts of peace and civilisation, and the welfare of our common humanity the world over."

In an article entitled "The Anglo-American Alliance and the Irish-Americans," by Rev. George McDermot, C.S.P.,[106] the writer opens his article with the following sentence:

"I was tempted to call the alliance proposed by certain persons between England and America 'the Chamberlain-American Alliance'; but stating this thought will answer the purpose of such a heading. I take the subject up as a parable, now that the Local Government Bill for Ireland has passed the Lower House. . . .

"I ask, where is the advantage to America to spring from such an alliance? I have spoken of the subject with reference to Mr. Chamberlain; I shall discuss it in the abstract and show, if space permits, that such an alliance is based on the suggestion of an immoral compact, and is intended for the promotion of a wicked policy, the main advantage of which would be found to rest with England. The idea stated is that the United States will give to England the part of the Philippines they do not mean to retain; and the justification for this is the Pecksniffian one that 'British Civilisation and British Rule will be for the benefit of the islanders.' It is hard to avoid reference to other islanders who have had a long experience of that rule and civilisation. We are informed in this publication, which is sometimes favoured with the lucubrations of Mr. Chamberlain, and never without glosses on his high policy by faithful hands, that 'if it is any advantage to England to own a new Asiatic possession she can probably add to the Empire without much trouble.' This bid for an alliance in pursuance of Mr. Chamberlain's aims is audacious in its candour. It is made at the very moment the 'touling' of the right honourable gentleman has become the subject of dignified and regretful criticism on the part

[105] *Canadian Magazine*, January, 1899.
[106] *Catholic World*, October, 1898.

of English public men and the raillery of the Continental press. The honour of the radical section of the Liberal party is saved. It was that section which stood by America in the Civil War, when the ruling and moneyed classes were equipping privateers to prey upon her commerce and trying to compel a recognition of the independence of the Confederacy. . . . "

The author closes with the following sentence:

"However, to pull the chestnuts out of the fire in China is one of the advantages America is to obtain by the proposed alliance; and to me, indeed, the putting of it forward affords the clearest indication that the Secretary for the Colonies, notwithstanding debating talents of no common order, is incapable of forming a policy, wider than the area of a borough, and unable to take the measure of relations and interests, difficulties and complications, larger than those which surround a scheme for lighting or paving a prosperous municipality in England."

Then I must not forget two quotations from articles by Mr. A. Maurice Low, "America's Debt to England"[107] where he says:

"An Anglo-American alliance—not merely an 'understanding,' but formal, definite alliance—I hope to see in the near future. It would mark an epoch in the world's history; it would mean the elevation, the happiness, the advancement of the whole world; it would bring us one step nearer the ideal. In the language of the British Secretary of State for Colonial affairs:

"'Our imagination must be fired when we contemplate the possibility of such a cordial understanding between the seventy million people of the United States and our fifty million Britons, an understanding which would guarantee peace and civilisation to the world.'"

In another article, entitled "Russia, England and the United States,"[108] he writes:

"In language, in thought, in habits, in manners, in morals, in religion there is nothing in common between the great mass of the people of the United States and the great mass of the people of the Czar's dominions. Our law is based on the common law of England; our literature is derived from the same inspiration; even when we have been foes our common blood has made our deeds and heroism soften the bitterness of war. Perry's victory on Lake Erie thrills the English boy as much as the recital of Broke's capture of the *Chesapeake* does the American. Only the other day American and British naval officers, fighting a common foe, fell side by side; and this was not the first time the blood of the two races had mingled facing the enemy; in fact, the Russian and the American are antagonistic. It is, as Senator Lodge points out, the conflict of the Slav and the Saxon—a conflict which has been waging for centuries, and must eventually be fought to the bitter end, until the freedom of the Saxon is so firmly planted that it can never be assailed, or the militarism of the Slav crushes the world under its iron heel and, for a second time, the 'Scourge of God' dominates."

---

[107] *Anglo-American Magazine,* March, 1899.
[108] *Forum,* October, 1899.

Last in time, but not in strength and eloquence of language, comes Mr. Stead, with a perfect torrent of ideas in favour of the quick nationalisation of the Anglo-Saxon peoples. His book must be read as a whole, and cannot be adequately portrayed by short quotations.[109]

I have now finished what I know to be an imperfect attempt to bring this great subject adequately before the mind of the reader. I must be satisfied merely to open it. The aim of the book is to show that the unification of the English-speaking peoples means the elevation and enlightenment of mankind, the mitigation of suffering, and the opening of new roads to human happiness. This is the mission of the race, and the twentieth century—the Anglo-Saxon Century—should behold its accomplishment.

To aid Anglo-Saxon union I appeal to philosophers, historians, and all other writers to espouse a cause which calls into exercise the best instincts and noblest impulses of mind and soul; I appeal to lawyers to combine in favour of a union which preserves and enlarges a system of jurisprudence, which, properly administered, means exact justice and true equality to all men; I appeal to individual priests and preachers everywhere to advocate a text which will draw men nearer to true religion; I appeal to all the Churches, whose holy mission is peace and good-will to the world; and I finally appeal to the organs of public opinion, individually and collectively: the Pulpit, the Press, the Bar, and the Stage, to help the great Anglo-Saxon peoples consummate their destiny in one combined effort to perform the duty with which God has charged them.

> "All power
> I give thee; reign for ever, and assume
> Thy merits; under thee, as Head Supreme,
> Thrones, Princedoms, Powers, Dominions,
> I reduce,"[110]

---

[109] *The Americanization of the World,* W.T. Stead.
[110] Paradise Lost, Book III.

INDEX

Lector House believes that a society develops through a two-fold approach of continuous learning and adaptation, which is derived from the study of classic literary works spread across the historic timeline of literature records. Therefore, we aim at reviving, repairing and redeveloping all those inaccessible or damaged but historically as well as culturally important literature across subjects so that the future generations may have an opportunity to study and learn from past works to embark upon a journey of creating a better future.

This book is a result of an effort made by Lector House towards making a contribution to the preservation and repair of original ancient works which might hold historical significance to the approach of continuous learning across subjects.

HAPPY READING & LEARNING!

LECTOR HOUSE LLP
E-MAIL: lectorpublishing@gmail.com